BECOME A
FEARLESS
WRITER

HOW TO STOP PROCRASTINATING, BREAK FREE OF SELF-DOUBT, AND BUILD A PROFITABLE CAREER

NINA HARRINGTON
NinaHarringtonDigital

BECOME A FEARLESS WRITER

Published by NinaHarringtonDigital.

TABLE OF CONTENTS

INTRODUCTION

THE $450,000 INVESTMENT THAT I ALMOST THREW AWAY BECAUSE OF PROCRASTINATION

Hello. My name is Nina Harrington and I am an award-winning author of 33 fiction and bestselling non-fiction books which have sold over 1.4 million copies worldwide in 23 languages. But I wasn't always so prolific or successful.

In 2013 I found myself in a rather special situation which was brilliant, challenging and very terrifying.

I had just signed a contract to write another three romance novels for Harlequin, when an exciting opportunity came out of the blue. Harlequin UK had brought in a dynamic and enthusiastic team of editors to create a new digital first publishing line called Carina UK.

Lightbulbs started popping over my head.

I had an idea for a novel length romantic crime book which was very different from the category romances I normally write, and was considering self-publishing the book as an experiment and learning experience.

Here was the chance to publish digital versions of my work, but with the full editorial and marketing support of a traditional publisher. Plus the royalty rates and publication package were very competitive and attractive.

So I sent a submission package into my editor, expecting it to take weeks for them to get back to me.

Oh no. In days, I had been asked to send in the full manuscript and two weeks after that first email, I was offered a three book contract with Carina UK. The editors loved the book and were excited and enthusiastic about working with me.

Brilliant! This was exactly what I had been working for since I gave up my career as a scientist in the pharmaceutical industry.

The chance to write romance and crime fiction full time had me jumping out of bed with a spring in my step!

And then the revision letter for my submission arrived, and the hard reality of my workload hit me smack in the face like a bucket of ice water.

I had already committed to write three 50,000 word romance novels for Harlequin that year, and now I had two 75,000 word Carina books to write in the next 12 months, plus a lot of work to do revising the first 80,000 word book for Carina. And the revisions had to be back in 2 weeks.

Two contracts. Six books. All different. All special. And since I always overwrite, I knew that in reality this probably meant creating almost half a million words in the next 12 months, not including detailed self-editing and revision cycles. [Did I mention that I am a perfectionist?]

Deep breath.

I knew that I could do it, if I managed my time and energy. But first I was going to have to face the greatest challenge of my life.

Every one of the books that I had written until that point had been hard won in a daily battle with self-inflicted self-sabotage and expert distraction seeking avoidance tactics.

In other words, *my chronic procrastination.*

Suddenly I felt as though I had been dropped into a whirlpool of self-doubt and limiting thoughts which kept playing on repeat inside my head.

- Every other writer gets it. Why can't I be perfect like everyone else?
- I had no idea that it would be this hard to build a career as a full-time writer.
- I don't know what to do to make the situation better.
- My life is out of control and I need help.
- I am frantically and relentlessly reading everyone's advice and listening to all of the gurus, and end up feeling that I am useless and failing, but I still want to do the best job I can.

The worst thing was, as a trained scientist, I knew perfectly well that these psychological barriers were totally self-generated, which of course made them even more frustrating and infuriating.

Now it was crunch time.

I ***had*** to do something about my procrastination once and for all, or stand the risk that either these six books were going to be produced in a big rush at the last minute, or I would miss my deadlines with my publishers.

Even worse. I would throw away the chance to finally write both crime and romance and see my work professionally edited and published.

This was my dream.

This was why I had taken a huge risk and left my well-paid job as an industrial scientist, and by that time had sacrificed about $450,000 of income and benefits on the altar of my fantasy of being a published fiction author.

I was dedicated to my work and was well compensated for the hours and the stress and pressure that came with a senior position. I loved the people I was working with and the company was great. I have always been a hard worker and gave my work my all.

So why did I walk away from my job without a publishing contract or guarantee of an income?

My creativity was, and still is, an essential part of my identity and also a way of expressing who I am as a person.

I wanted to get to know that other side of me which reflected the writer, who I knew deep inside I had the potential to become.

The alternative was to carry on with paid employment and go to my retirement party with the stories and characters burning inside of me, untold.

It had taken me six years of hard work and millions of words and daily practice to win that first publishing contract with a traditional publisher.

Now I was at my wits end.

I had to crush this procrastination if there was any chance of completing these six manuscripts, editing and then revising them in the next 12 months.

There was no choice.

I needed a battle plan – and I needed one fast.

Procrastination was not going to win, not this time; there was simply too much at stake to allow that to happen.

My goals were simple. I had to explore and develop powerful tools which would allow me to:
- increase my productivity so I could write more and progressively better books in the time available

- eliminate time wasting and distractions so that I would move forward on my main writing project every day and stay on schedule
- have a life outside writing, where I could relax knowing that I have achieved my daily targets
- prevent stress, overwhelm and burnout, and build a system where I could stop worrying about word count and get back to enjoying the writing and having fun.

What I found was that there is an overwhelming amount of productivity related material to wade through.

Business and personal development gurus have created multiple DVD sets and coaching services galore, covering procrastination and time management and these are on sale worldwide.

Add to that list the numerous training courses you can buy online for large sums which promise that your procrastination will be a thing of the past.

Plus the many thousands of books, articles and blog posts with the top three, five, seven, ten etc. tips which will cure your procrastination.

The subject soon becomes totally unmanageable - or another excellent form of procrastination.

It was time to cut a clear path through the woods.

What did I learn?

It is possible to create a writing career where there is less frustration and anxiety, more fun and less stress every day.

But just like any other craft, the better your tools the easier the work.

This book is a compilation of the key concepts and tools that I borrowed from a wide range of sources, and how I used these techniques to transform my writing life.

Important Note: Although I am a Ph.D. scientist, I am **not** an expert or trained in any kind of therapy. If you suffer from chronic symptoms in any area of self-belief such as perfectionism, then I would urge you to research the options in depth, and seek professional help if this is the best way forward for you. Everyone is different but crippling self-doubt seems to be a common pestilence which impacts many writers at every stage of their life and career. Don't be scared to get some help.

What I **can** do is share some of the tools and techniques that I have tested in the real world as a professional writer, in the hope that you will find them useful.

What you will learn in this book

This book is divided into the five parts which describe the comprehensive MAGIC system.

Over the past few years I have personally tested every technique to make sure that they work when I need them most.

M. MOTIVATION and the Success MINDSET. Finding your True North. Everything starts with your WHY. *Everything.*

A. ACCEPTANCE of your current situation and your unique strengths, and the truth about the underlying mental brain chatter holding you back. Self-Awareness about WHO you are now, and how you came to be here, and WHO you want to become. Limiting self-beliefs and self-talk will always be with you, but you can control them and come out fighting with a powerful feeling of self-worth and self-mastery. Your unique strengths will guide the way.

G. The **GAP** between where you are at this moment in your life and where you want to go. Your personal list of dream results and objectives. Your future self. Working backwards from the end result so that you know what steps you need to take to create your unique ideal future.

I. IMPLEMENTATION. Lists and dream objectives are useless without action. Think of this as an experiment. A fun game, where you are trying out new things. WHAT you are going to do, and in what order, so that you can work smarter and faster. Execution and consistency are everything

C. COMMITMENT. WHEN are you going to get started on your Implementation plan? We all have amazing ideas for projects and stories but how many of us bring those ideas to life? You may have to develop new routines and that can take time, so the sooner you can get started the better.

By working through the MAGIC system, I was able to break down the workload into chunks and focus on my WHY whenever things got tough. New daily routines and working practices followed, and I have been using this process ever since.

By the end of the book you will have the tools and techniques and the confidence you need to break out of the procrastination cycle and transform your productivity, so that you can share your stories and writing with your readers.

"It's never too late to be what you might have been."
Attributed to George Eliot

STEP ONE. MOTIVATION AND THE SUCCESS MINDSET

I don't know about you, but after an hour or two on the internet, my brain is totally buzzing with ideas for new projects, business information about how to launch a start-up enterprise, and amazing insights into story craft, publishing models and technology.
It is like going down a never ending tunnel!

Somehow we have to process everything that we have seen and heard and make sense of it all, so we can integrate that new information into our work as creative entrepreneurs.

It is exhausting.

All of these new ideas are then stacked up on top of all of the *other* things we believe we *should* be doing but haven't got around to yet, and all of the other writers seem to know what they are doing.

Plus you may have a day job and a home life to deal with.

In fact, it is so overwhelming that you can have brain freeze and just push all the exciting, challenging and interesting ideas to one side because they are too much to deal with ... right now.

And we know what that means! We get trapped in a never ending loop of frustration and self-doubt which saps our self-esteem and self-confidence. This makes it even tougher to return to a positive and dynamic state of mind.

In the first step of the MAGIC system we are going to focus on how to leverage the power of deep motivation and crystal clear objectives, through understanding:

- Why so many of us put things off.
- How to master self-motivation.
- Clarity. Finding your why.
- What is your definition of success?
- Life planning.
- The psychology of motivation.
- External and internal motivation.
- Goals vs end results.
- The success mindset.

"Follow your heart but listen to your head." Steve Jobs

WHY DO SO MANY OF US PUT THINGS OFF?

There are some precious and rare mornings when we wake up with a spring in our step, bursting with energy and excitement about the amazing things that we are going to achieve that day. We cannot wait to get started!

But then there are the other kind of days, when we could happily pull the covers back over our heads and forget about getting up at all. It is only the threat of poverty or social media photos of what we look like eating lunch in our pyjamas, that forces us into a sluggish form of action.

Why can't we hold onto that enthusiasm and apply it to every project?

Surely we don't want to sink into that feeling of self-loathing that comes with lethargy and procrastination?

Kevin Kruse gives a quote from Dr. Joseph Ferrari from an interview with the American Psychological Association:

"We all put tasks off, but my research has found that 20 percent of U.S. men and women are chronic procrastinators...that's higher than the number of people diagnosed with clinical depression or phobias, two tendencies many people know about."

So why do so many of us procrastinate and what can we do about it?

TIME TO DISPEL SOME COMMON MYTHS ABOUT MOTIVATION AND PROCRASTINATION

If you go to any bookstore, online or otherwise, you will find a bewildering range of textbooks and business management guides which all claim to have the answer to the problem of procrastination in topics such as weight loss, career development, competitive sports, and sales and marketing.

The subject soon becomes totally unmanageable, or another excellent form of time spinning, but very few of these books are action based, and in many cases they repeat the same myths, which are both untrue and without the scientific evidence to support them.

MYTH NUMBER ONE: PROCRASTINATORS ARE LAZY

There is one myth that is repeated in many of these books and training videos, that we need to quash right now.

Procrastination is not laziness or lying to yourself.

Just the opposite. We care so much about our work and it means so much to us, that we have become experts in applying avoidance tactics in response to a whole range of fears and anxieties.

I believe that we often put things off because we love what we do and passionately understand how important our writing is to our life, self-identity and our future careers as published authors.

MYTH NUMBER TWO: WE DON'T WANT IT ENOUGH

This could apply if you are working on the wrong project for the wrong reasons. Most of the time, we procrastinate because we care desperately about taking our writing to the next level and making it a success. We not only want the project to be a success but need it to be!

That tension creates the internal stress that drives the anxiety when we are putting in the hours, but end up having nothing to show for all of that work.

MYTH NUMBER THREE: YOU JUST NEED MORE WILLPOWER

Wrong. Willpower is both unreliable and fallible, since it relies on daily and deliberate injections of positive and dynamic thinking and personal drive.

This is both unsustainable and exhausting. Willpower alone will not get you through the challenges of time and energy management when your writing has to take a lower priority when confronted with daily modern life.

HOW TO MASTER SELF-MOTIVATION

Let's make one thing clear.

I believe that everyone, whether they are a writer or not, deserves to live a meaningful life which is bursting with excitement and positive energy.

A life full of fun and hard work, which is strategically aligned to your personal vision for your future identity and lifestyle.

Do you want to break the monotonous cycle of eating and sleeping and working, and spending hours in front of your TV, playing games or on social media, and then feeling guilty because you should have invested that time in a creative project?

Yes? Then let's get to work.

THE PSYCHOLOGY OF SELF-MOTIVATION

We all know about motivation don't we? After all, we fiction writers spend hours working on the motivation and background histories for the characters in our books.

The psychology of our own motivation is quite different but equally important.

One key aspect is whether you believe that **you** are in control of your life and your career.

Ellen Langer said in her book "*Mindfulness*" that "*when you perceive choice then you perceive motivation*".

This concept that you can control and create the future you want, is at the heart of self-motivation.

SELF-EMPOWERMENT AND SELF-DETERMINATION

Self-Determination Theory is a broad psychological framework used to study human motivation and personality.

The theory focuses on three basic psychological needs which can be described as:

#1. Autonomy and Self-Empowerment. You are able to express yourself freely and make your own decisions about what matters in your life. You have the luxury of choice about what you do, and how and where you do it.

#2. Competence and Self-Efficacy. You have the necessary time, skillset, knowledge and training to carry out any task you want to complete and master it.

#3. Relatedness. This has to do with the relationships we have around us with our loved ones, friends and social groups. Our support structure and human connection is important and shouldn't be neglected.

If any of these three psychological needs is missing or unsupported, then self-determination theory tells us that we won't be able to become fully self-motivated.

USING THE POWER OF SELF-DETERMINATION TO DRIVE SELF-MOTIVATION

Consider the key aspects of this framework.

- Do you feel that you have full control and are deeply motivated about what projects to work on?
- Do you feel fully invested and in control of whatever project you are working on and know that you can own it and drive it forwards?
- When you start work on a project have you ever felt that you did not know what you were doing and did not have the skills to complete it or the will to learn those skills?

- Do your family and friends support you in your work as a writer? Do you have a network of pals who understand why you do what you do and are they there for you?

As you answer these questions, do you feel that you have the power to control your own future?

If the answer to any of those questions made you sigh out loud and shake your head, then you are not alone.

The key thing to realise is that you can become self-empowered and develop rock-solid confidence in your abilities and your future purpose-led life.

Change Starts from the ***inside out***.

Everything starts with your Why. *Everything*!

"When you put your "stamp" on things and take ownership of them, you are taking things out of the hands of fate and putting them into your own hands. Success or failure is all on you. Not on the will or whim of others. "Let's see what happens" is the anti-thesis of this ideal. The self-determined person will make it happen." Dan Blank

CLARITY: FINDING YOUR DEEP PURPOSE

You have probably heard the old saying: "*Where there is a will, there is a way.*"

You can push through anything if you know and understand the specific objective that you want to achieve.

Nothing is going to get in your way – including yourself!

You become the best version of you.

The tools and techniques of project planning and your story craft skills are the essential components that will drive your writing career and your business, but your deep internal motivation is the fuel, the gas, the power that will propel you forwards.

Your WHY is the roadmap to where you want to go.

No matter how many times you rev the engine and how fast you drive, if you don't know where you are going you will end up either going around in circles, or racing down a narrow lane heading towards a dead end.

Your WHY will help you to find your way back on track and get to your final destination.

MINDSET EXERCISE: THE VIRTUAL PLANK TEST

In his book, *The Now Habit*, Neil Fiore describes a thought experiment where he invites us to use our imagination and carry out a simple test. I have shamelessly borrowed the concept and adapted it for this example.

Here is the task. All you have to do is walk down a flat, safe, solid wooden board which is four inches thick, a foot wide and maybe three or 4 four feet long. It will not warp or twist when you walk on it.

Situation #1: Place the wooden board flat on the floor.

You can skip, run, and hop, salsa if you want, but you have to walk down the entire length of the board from one end to the other.

It only takes a few seconds. No stress. No problems. All good.

This board represents the two rough pages that you are going to write today over coffee or tea. Two sides of paper are about 500 words depending on the size of your font and your writing style.

Situation #2: Lift the board and prop it up with a solid block under each end of the board, so that the board is about 12 inches off the ground and you have to step up to stand on it.

The 500 words are now the synopsis for a new story idea which you have to submit tomorrow to an editor so that they can approve a new contract.

Don't forget. You can take one step back down onto the floor at any time.

How do you feel about the board now? Um?

Maybe you should change your shoes? Or wait until someone is around to hold your hand, in case you fall those 12 inches.

But you can do it. It took a long time to build up the courage but it was actually not too bad.

Situation #3: We lift the board and prop it across two solid chairs at hip height.

How do we feel about walking down that solid piece of wood now?

Those 500 words are the submission letter to a famous literary agent or a query letter to a big publisher, who might **reject** you! Or might even find out that you are a fraud or an imposter.

Different situation.

Now all you are thinking about is the fear of falling and the distance between the board and the hard floor, and the potential outcomes from stepping onto the chair and then walking down that plank of wood.

- If you fell off you could hurt yourself. Even getting up there to try is a mistake.
- If you break your ankle you wouldn't be able to drive or walk the dog or go to work or...

What is Nina thinking?

I am thinking that we are now totally focusing on the fear and imagining the worst case scenario for the outcome, and all of the negative feelings around those poor outcomes.

The task is still 500 words and the equivalent of two pages.

500 words!

You probably text and email more than 500 words every day without thinking or worrying, because you have not layered and associated those words with a particular negative feeling or end result.

So what happens in real life?

We stand on the edge of the board, tottering in our heels but too frightened to take that first step onto the board to get across – until something pushes us forwards.

The deadline for a contest or a submission deadline is next week and the book has been sitting there for months.

There is a fire burning behind your back and the only way to escape the flames is to somehow get across this board to the other side. There might even be someone pushing you.

You *have* to do it. No choice. It is too late to do anything else. The time pressure is enormous and you have run out of options.

So you get down onto your knees and grab onto the board, close your eyes and inch your way along the board, ignoring the fiery pit beneath you, praying to your choice of deity that you can make it across in one piece.

So of course you do the work, but at 2am on a school night.

At the end you feel exhausted and deflated because you got the job done just in time.

But was it your best work?

Was it a true reflection of your talent and skill?

Probably not. You are emotionally exhausted, and it certainly was not a positive experience.

You have just created a negative memory associated with that task.

So what happens next time you are in the same situation?

That negative memory kicks in and you feel even less likely to get started.

This cycle of negative associations with your work will continue unless you do something to break the loop and replace that negativity with a positive emotional experience.

STAKES AND OUTCOMES MEAN THAT *CONTEXT IS EVERYTHING*

All of the fear is about the context our brains create around the simple task of writing those 500 words.

So what happens when we are faced with a big task such as writing a book or submitting our work to a literary agent or publisher?

Anxiety. Fear. Terror!

This is when we step back from a great idea, because we are afraid of future negative consequences.

So we self-sabotage. To keep safe. To protect ourselves from rejection and failure, or huge success, which can be pretty scary too.

So we watch TV or videos of kittens on YouTube and spend hours on social media instead.

It is way too easy to go backwards when we hit that brick wall of a challenge where something does not work as we had expected, and the constant chipping away at our self-confidence finally creates a hole where self-doubt and fear can slip inside.

All we can hear is the negative brain chatter telling us that we are fools for even trying.

Even worse, that failure feeds into a cycle of more self-doubt.

The project feels doomed and no longer worth our time, so we turn to another idea, which has not been contaminated with the feelings of failure and frustration.

Only the cycle repeats itself until we give up entirely, exhausted and demoralised.

So how do you build a fantastic solid bridge over the valley of death underneath that virtual wooden board?

You find something which is bigger and more powerful than the fear, and it lies on the other side of that bridge.

The bridge is made up from the solid foundations of your deep internal motivation, your mojo and your personal power and drive.

You are going to stride out across the bridge.

And below you can hear the screams of all the people who are lying on their death beds, full of regret and bitterness that they never wrote that book which was their hearts' desire, or told someone they loved them.

They allowed fear to take control of their lives.

And now it is too late to be the person they knew in their hearts they were meant to be.

Not you!

You are going to focus on what you want, and you are going to want it so badly that it will pull you across that bridge, no matter how high it is above the ground, by the power of positive energy and enthusiasm and passion.

You are going to find your deep purpose and use it like a James Bond jetpack to power you across that bridge. Legs akimbo, skirts or trousers in the air.

That doesn't matter, because now you have taken the control back from fear.

Now you have the power to create the life and career you want.

To paraphrase the old Polish expression, *this is your circus and these are your monkeys.* Time to get the show on the road!

APPLYING THE PSYCHOLOGY OF MOTIVATION

MOTIVATIONAL DRIVERS

Successful authors and entrepreneurs in every kind of business understand in a deep way what they want and why they want it.

Yes, they are resilient and hardworking, but they focus all of that energy and determination on the one single direction they want to go.

That direction comes from a deep and enduring sense of self-motivation. Driven by the **why**.

Every author struggles with productivity, but your talent and challenges are unique.

By revolutionising what you think about your strengths and your capabilities, you can get back to what matters to you, and create a profitable writing career where there is **less stress, more joy and delight in the work** and **much more personal satisfaction.**

Willpower does not work without a supporting belief system.

Neither does the latest app or piece of software – they are tools to help you manage your project list. But they certainly are not designed to help you get to your life's purpose.

EMOTIONAL TRIGGERS

This technique links your feelings to powerful internal desires that are so important to us that we will take action to make them happen.

For example, think of a time when you were totally motivated. Perhaps you wanted to finish building a doll's house for your daughter in time for Christmas morning, or learn to drive and pass your test before you went to college. Or perhaps you were working on a novel and would receive the advance royalty payment when you delivered the manuscript. That money would pay for your family holiday.

Each of these examples had two elements associated with it:

- There was a specific deadline and time limit.
- You were working towards a specific benefit, and each of these was linked to an emotional experience. You wanted to share the joy on a little girl's face when she saw that doll's house, or feel the sense of liberation and freedom that came with being able to drive a car anywhere you wanted.

That emotional trigger can make all of the difference to your motivation to complete a project within a fixed deadline.

Completing even a small part of a project like writing a novel can make you feel more: satisfied, loved, rewarded, in control, empowered and autonomous.

You decided to do this and you did it! You made it happen.

The good news is this; you already have everything you need to develop powerful self-motivation and it won't cost you more than a couple of hours, at most, of your quiet time.

So how do you make the shift and satisfy your three basic psychological needs of autonomy, competence and confidence and the community support?

You take the time to work through all of your ideas and dreams and hopes for your future and then define your end destination.

The first step to powerful self-motivation is defining the end destination in such a crystal clear way that you will be able to describe it to another person in a one sentence. Goals or tactics are simply steps along the path towards that final destination.

WHO ARE YOU COMPETING AGAINST?

You should only compete with one person: *yourself*.

The real journey is only against yourself and your unrealized potential.

TAKING THE MIRROR CHALLENGE

This is what the musician Jay Z means when he raps, "*I look in the mirror, my only opponent*".

Rather than competing against the next person, you can visualise your future self. Actor Matthew McConaughey chases his ideal self, ten years in the future. He says, "*Every day, every week, every month, and every year of my life, my hero is always 10 years away. I'm never going to beat my hero. ...That's just fine with me, because it keeps me with somebody to keep on chasing.*"

When you compete with yourself, you won't be lured into competition with other people and their values and needs.

Only you can decide what really matters to you.

WHAT IS YOUR EXTERNAL MOTIVATION?

One powerful example of external motivation is income:

- You might have had a childhood dream of seeing your name on a printed book in a bookshop, or the kudos of being included on a bestseller list.

- Paying the bills. Simple as that. It is writing or getting a job outside your home. There is no shame in wanting to write books that sell well. This is your business after all and you are investing your time, your energy and money in your business so you should be rewarded for that. But may I suggest that it is not the money you want, it is what you can do with that money. Money gives you choices.

- Lots of writers pay school fees to give their kids a great education and home life. In these tough economic times being able to keep your kids in private schools and a university education is not easy. They write to give their family and loved ones a better life.

- Dream holidays in wonderful locations with the family and friends having fun. And you paid for that by working through your procrastination and creating words other people want to buy. I love the Greek Islands. Two weeks in the Ionian acts as a powerful motivation for me.

- Having enough income to be able to donate to charitable causes and share your income with those who need it.

And then there is the big question.

WHAT IS YOUR INTERNAL MOTIVATION?

What is your purpose? Your obsession? What do you truly want and do you want it badly enough?

For me, I know there are stories burning inside of me which will never be read unless I write them. I do not want to go to my grave full of regret and my dreams unfulfilled.

Not going to happen.

In 2002 I gave up a well-paid job to write full time – without a contract, but I knew that I had to give this my best shot. Not a brag, but I have *"walked the talk"* about sacrificing a lot to live my passion.

For example:

- You might want to prove to your old English teacher or your family that they were wrong when they said that your dyslexia would make it impossible for you to ever write more than your name.

- You might want to prove to yourself that you can finish a book even if you never have it published, or you do not want it published.

- You might want to write a children's or YA book so your children can read it and this will be your legacy to them.

- Your talent has the potential to provide an income for the rest of your life, which will enable you to travel the world in comfort and visit places you only dreamt about.

Every one of us has our own personal drivers.

Where do you want to go?

Do you have a vision for where your writing will take you?

"The greatest achievement in life is to have the ability to create the world around you so that it matches the dreams in your head." Mike Dillon.

WHAT IS SUCCESS?

Answer. **Success is what YOU define it to be.**

The media may project an image of success linked to celebrity and glamour and millions in the bank and all of the other material trappings of wealth or kudos, but for most creative entrepreneurs personal success means something very different.

Personal achievement against the odds.

Many of the authors I know would define success as being able to overcome their personal battles on a daily basis so that they can achieve their long held aspiration of being a published author, and sharing their stories and writing with readers around the world.

Earning More Money

Simply earning enough to work from home and see your children grow up in a secure, happy and loving home, and being part of a family and a community may be part of your idea of true success.

Living a Better Life

To other people, success means having the freedom to travel the world and being able to choose what to do with their life every day.

Once you have defined the end results that you want to achieve in your life, you know what success will look like when you get there.

HOW TO DIG DEEP AND FIND YOUR WHY

"The bigger the why, the easier the how." Jim Rohn

If you can leverage the power of a deep emotionally driven reason for being a successful author, then you can push through any of the roadblocks that life and your career will throw at you.

It all comes down to this. **What is YOUR definition of success?**

Do you want your writing to pay so that you can give up the day job and work from home?

Or does success mean the kudos and personal delight of seeing your name in print? Or the challenge of proving to yourself that you can do this?

If you are a single title, one book a year author and happy to stay that way, that's amazing.

On the other hand, if you want to see your book on supermarket shelves and be interviewed on daytime TV chat shows, that's great and good luck with that too.

You have to know what you want out of this crazy mad career and be brutally honest and open to that truth.

In ***Smarter Faster Better***, the journalist Charles Duhigg weaves together case studies and scientific research and stories to illustrate the importance of mindset to achievement in multiple fields.

"To teach ourselves to be self-motivated more easily, we need to learn to see all choices not just as expressions of control but also of affirmations of all values and goals. Asking why is how we link small tasks to larger aspirations....Motivation is triggered by making choices that demonstrate to ourselves that we are in control—and that we are moving towards goals that are meaningful. It's that feeling of self-determination that gets us going.

You have to have a crystal clear understanding of the deep internal motivation. This is fundamental. If you don't know what your motivation is, you will struggle to maintain your work when things get tough." Charles Duhigg

MOTIVATION EXERCISE: FROM DREAMING TO DOING

Objective: To create a mental white space where you are totally clear about why you want to work on a creative project and where it fits into your life.

This is a six-step process which should take about an hour at most.

STEP #1. DOWNLOAD YOUR BRAIN ONTO PAPER

Get comfy with a pad of paper and a pen, take a deep breath and brain dump onto paper every single thing that you have always dreamt of accomplishing in your life and work.

Then add in the challenges which are causing you concern and feeding your anxiety, plus all of the items on your to do list.

And I mean *everything*.

From what is happening in your home life, your work and your writing, to bank interest rates and world peace if that is keeping you awake at night.

Write fast and hold nothing back.

Keep going and let all of your dreams and hopes and fears and struggles flow down your pen and onto the paper.

Remember - the only person who will see this list is you.

STEP #2. WHAT YOU CAN PERSONALLY CONTROL

Get up and find your favourite refreshment, then sit back down and go through that list and put a line through everything that you cannot personally control and have the power to drive to completion at this moment in your life.

I am really sorry to have to tell you, but the manned space flight programme is probably not going to accept your application, so if astronaut training is on the list, it may have to go in the standby plan. You cannot personally control and drive that project to completion at this moment.

Be strong.

You cannot control the state of publishing and reader tastes.

You cannot personally control the current job market in your town and the world economy or political landscape.

You cannot control other people's attitudes and feelings which are feeding your negative attitudes and doubts. So what if your sister in law thinks your paranormal erotic romance is smut and refuses to call you a writer?

Let it go.

You are not going to change her mind.

In fact from now on you are going to say that it is not just smut but the finest trashiest smut which your readers are going to adore. Then imagine offering her a lift to the supermarket in your new Bentley convertible which you bought with your big pile of money your romance books are bringing in every month. And if this has not happened yet cut out a picture of some aspirational object or dream location and stick it on your monitor.

You cannot control how people feel and think.

You cannot allow your life and dreams to be crushed or held hostage by other people's expectations.

Refuse to allow that to happen. You have the right to those life dreams.

Why do you have to limit this list to things inside your control?

You have to feel confident at this point that you are capable of achieving your chosen dream or end result, even if that means overcoming the challenges in your life at this time.

If you can control the outcome then your dream stays on the list.

STEP #3. HOW DOES EACH ITEM ON THE LIST MAKE YOU FEEL?

Next, read what you have left on your list and think about how each idea makes you feel.

Don't think about cost or how you could make it happen, just focus on your emotional response to the idea.

Does that thing excite you and inspire you or is it a bit, well.... meh?

It could be a good thing or even a great and noble thing, but if it does not inspire you and make your heart leap just at the thought of being able to achieve it, cross it out.

STEP #4. CHALLENGE YOUR POWER LIST

You should now have a few things left on your wrecked and scribbled sheets of paper, which have not been crossed through.

Take a new sheet of paper and copy over what is left, adding just a line or two about each project or end result.

Then sit and stare at your new list.

It might have one item on it or twenty.

How many does not matter because this is your personal power list.

Now ask yourself these questions for every single one of the items on the new list:

- Can you visualise inside your head how your life would be different if you completed the project and achieved that end result? Yes or no.
- Does even thinking about that project and the end result make you grin in delight, so that you feel excited and heart-thumpingly invigorated? Yes or no.
- Would that project make you jump out of bed in the morning at 5am so you can work on it for 2 hrs before your family get up? Or keep you working until 2am on a school day? Yes or no.

If you answer no to any of these questions – you know what to do. Cross it out.

STEP #5. DIGGING DEEPER

You should now have a small list of ideas and dream projects and ambitions, or maybe just one, which mean a lot to you and which you feel you have the power to control and drive forwards. They have to be powerful and real and honest.

Now it is time to take a hard look at what is left and ask yourself the reasons why these items truly matter to you so very much.

I suspect you already know the answers, but try to think through each question with the first reply that comes into your head.

Don't overthink it or try and come up with a clever answer. This is for you, nobody else.

Why do you want to achieve this end result?

Example. I want to write a crime novel because I would love to see a book that I had written in the bookshop.

Why do you **really** want to achieve this ambition?

Example. I want to earn enough money working from home so that I can stay at home with my family instead of leaving them to go out to work each day.

What do you **really, really,** want to achieve this ambition?

Example. I have wanted to write fiction since I was a teenager when I made up stories for my little brother but I went down another path at college and then a full time job. I feel if I don't do this now, I will never have another chance to prove to myself that I can be a writer and published author. This is who I was meant to be and until now I feel that I have never been allowed to express myself and show what I am capable of.

Keep asking why, even if it becomes emotional along the way.

Drill down and keep on drilling down, until you reach the real answer.

There is no wrong or right answer. Only the truth. *Your truth*. You don't have to tell anyone – this is totally yours. Unique and special.

STEP #6. DECIDE ON WHO YOU WANT TO BECOME

What you now have is your master power list.

What I call my *"Fire in the Belly"* list.

This is what will fly you across that valley of fear.

It could be anything, including health, home, family and where you want to go in your writing.

But there is one final stage which is critically important.

Do you truly believe that you can reach that final destination and create a new identity for yourself?

You have to decide to start moving towards the person who you want to become. Because there is no doubt about it. You will be different in so many ways.

Are you ready to be the person who will have reached the final destination, or destinations, on your list?

Yes? Then let's get moving.

BONUS CONTENT

Go to **http://ninaharrington.com/Bonuses/** to

Download a Free Copy of this Motivation Exercise

THE SUCCESS MINDSET

It doesn't matter whether you are writing as a side hustle or fulltime, your creative work is either:

#1. A hobby which you enjoy doing for your personal entertainment and creative expression, or

#2. A small business where you sell what you create, so that other people can enjoy it, while you generate income.

Only you can decide the answer to that question.

If you want to write as a hobby, I hope that this book helps you to be more productive and develop your skills.

The remainder of this section focuses on the second option: You are writing to generate an income which will give you the freedom and choice to live how and where you want.

There is one common thread that links all of these success statements and it is this: In order to achieve the success that you have defined for yourself, you have to change or shift the way you think about your creative work.

The key to achieving any sort of success in the current economic and social climate is to build an unstoppable entrepreneurial mindset.

YOU ARE A CREATIVE ENTREPRENEUR BUILDING A START-UP BUSINESS

I know this idea offends many artistic writers, but in the current publishing world, the hard truth is that if you want to create the kind of success that will sustain your life's ambitions, then you have to pivot into thinking of your work as being not only an artistic expression and a craft, but also a valuable and beneficial product you are going to be able to sell as part of a business.

My fiction has been traditionally published and I have self-published both crime fiction and non-fiction books.

Over the past 15 years the gap between these two publishing models has narrowed enormously.

Traditionally published authors now invest heavily in exactly the same business tools and techniques as self-published authors, in order to build an audience and optimise book sales.

WHAT DO I MEAN BY A START-UP BUSINESS?

For most people, their experience of business is that you do work for someone and then you get paid for that work.

It can be tough for creative entrepreneurs such as writers to suddenly take on a new identity: business owner.

But that is precisely what you are already doing.

You are investing your time, your energy and your money in an enterprise to produce creative work which someone else is going to purchase and enjoy and benefit from.

I have carried out extensive research on how the most successful authors and other creative entrepreneurs manage their time and become truly prolific and productive.

After reading hundreds of articles, books and blog posts, I believe those entrepreneurs who built a profitable business from their writing, share common attributes and mind sets.

SUCCESSFUL CREATIVE ENTREPRENEURS SHARE SIX KEY QUALITIES

#1. Total Personal Control

They accept they are sole traders who have to take on all of the roles of a traditional business but with a twist. They can run their business the way they want to, where and how they want. This could mean they outsource some aspects of their publishing business to other people with the technical and design skills required for the business to succeed.

#2. Focus on One Niche and Build Authority

These entrepreneurs are bootstrappers, with limited or zero budgets, who have to become creative to achieve the results they are looking for. They focus on one idea and one market and niche, and aim to dominate that market for the products they want to specialise in.

#3. Risk Averse. Validate First.

These entrepreneurs are very risk averse. They don't waste their time or energy on projects until they have validated that there is a market for their work. If there is no market for the product they plan to write or make, then they don't invest their time on the project. It is as simple as that. They test the market before starting any new project.

#4. Invest Time in Building a Platform for their Brand

A brilliant product will not be a success if nobody knows it exists. Building a website and a public face to the world, connecting with the ideal audience for their product and growing relationships with influencers in their niche is critical to their success. By staying authentic to who they are, these entrepreneurs know they are creating a long term career through genuine relationships with customers and fellow creatives. Building a mailing list of potential purchasers is a very important metric for any start-up business.

#5. Understand the Importance of Working Productively

These solo entrepreneurs look at every creative project as a "Start-Up" microbusiness where they have to work ridiculously hard, but in a highly focused way to achieve maximum results in the time available.

The time management techniques of corporate business are not going to work. SMART** goals are great for finite corporate team projects, but they simply don't fit the way most creative authors work.

A one size fits all approach is not the way to go.

Instead, successful authors take a step back and invest time in looking at the big picture first, and create an overall strategy and plan before diving into the detailed tactics.

They know the end result and can define the end experience they are looking for at the start.

**[Specific, Measurable, Attainable, Realistic and Timed]

#6. Accept they have to own and master all aspects of their business operation so they stay in complete control

This means they accept they are the only ones who will drive new product design and development, and distribute, sell, market and promote their work.

They run the finance department, tech support and do all of the admin.

Once they have reached a scale where the income is coming in, then they might consider bringing in more people to join their team, or outsourcing, but at the start they are going to do what needs to be done to drive their business forward and create results.

THE ENTREPRENEURIAL MINDSET FOR AUTHORS AND CREATIVE ENTREPRENEURS

Building an entrepreneurial mindset is at the heart of every successful author.

They shift their mindset to think differently about how they use their mental and physical energy every minute of their day.

The good news is that you don't need to buy the latest app for your smart phone or some expensive software to shift your mental attitudes and beliefs towards becoming a creative entrepreneur. Everything you need you already own. *Your brain.*

For twenty years, my research has shown that the view you adopt for yourself profoundly affects the way that you lead your life. It can determine whether you become the person you want to be and whether you accomplish the things you value. Dr Carol S. Dweck

"**Mindset**" is a concept described by psychologist Carol Dweck following decades of research on achievement and personal success.

A person's mindset refers to their collection of beliefs, ways of thinking, assumptions and attitudes that determine their outlook on life and how they would respond to a certain situation.

There are two basic types of mindset:

In a **fixed mindset**, people believe that they have been given a certain fixed amount of intelligence or talent.

People with a fixed mindset are out to prove themselves every day and get very defensive when someone suggests they have made a mistake — they measure themselves by their failures.

In a **growth mindset**, people believe that their abilities can be developed through study and hard work and that intelligence and talent are just the starting point. This view creates a love of learning and a resilience to overcome challenges with positive energy. They believe that they can realise their true potential and are in control.

People with growth mindset show resilience when they've made an error and become more motivated to work harder and develop the skills needed to succeed in that task.

You can imagine how much difference it makes to your life, and your potential, if you believe you have a growth mindset rather than a fixed mindset.

Your mindset is a powerful asset, and developing a growth mindset can produce sudden and profound changes in your life.

"A growth mindset isn't simply a positive mindset. This isn't just about being happy. It is about a fundamental belief that you can grow, learn and change for the better – through failure and success alike. This mindset motivates you to try, to reflect, to get back up, to ask for help and to learn. Ultimately changed minds is what brings about a big change." Richard Branson

The good news is that modern neuroscience has shown that not only is the human brain capable of adapting and changing in response to our activities, but the more stimulus we give it, the sharper it becomes. When we learn new things and enjoy new experiences, the tiny neural connections inside the brain multiply and branch out to create more powerful networks.

Our brains are capable of sustained growth and increased capacity, irrespective of our age or past history and the genes we were born with.

Not only is a "growth mindset" possible, it can actually produce significant benefits to our long term mental health.

The conclusions are clear: no matter where you are starting from, you can develop the mental attitudes and strengths which will allow you to prosper as a creative entrepreneur.

"Adjusting our mindset for success is always at least half the battle. In the case of overcoming our fears, rather than being overcome by them, – it is 99% a war waged in our own head."
Connie Kerbs

PROGRAMMING YOUR MIND FOR SUCCESS

"Success is no accident. Living an incredible life is no accident. You have to do it on purpose. And it starts with knowing exactly what it is that you want to achieve, knowing why you want to achieve it, knowing the kind of person that you need to become in order to make it happen and then programming your mind to make it happen." Carrie Green. Tedx Manchester.

A Growth Mindset>>Positive Self-Talk>>Motivation

BECOME HUNGRY FOR SUCCESS

Develop a terrific sense of urgency in everything that you do!

I don't want to sound negative or depressing, but we do only have one life and a finite amount of time to accomplish everything that we want to do in this life. We don't know how long we have, and we should feel grateful for every new day that we are given.

Because one thing is certain: time is our number one asset. It is up to every one of us to use every hour as best we can.

The good news is there has never been a better time to start a business as a creative entrepreneur.

Think of it this way.

If you had to make enough money every month to pay all your living expenses, what would you need to do? Starting right now. Today!

Would you combine paid freelance writing or admin work with creative writing for example?

Leverage the power of a start-up business mentality to fuel your creativity about how you can run a business as a solo entrepreneur.

You are going to drive this. You should not have to rely on anyone else around you to help you drive this business to profitability.

You have to *own* it. You are it!

The good news is that we now have the online tools and techniques and software facilities to run a small business from anywhere in the world where there is a good internet connection.

The advancement in technology and the scope for solo entrepreneurs to build a brand and an author platform, at very low cost or free of charge, are truly astonishing.

One thing however is critical. The entrepreneurial mindset is not something you can buy or lease.

You have to be able to say:

- **This is why this project matters, and**
- **This is what I am going to do to make it happen.**

Once you have those two powerful aspects clear and written down, then you are ready to face the challenges that will try and thwart you.

"You are the master of your destiny. You can influence, direct and control your own environment. You can make your life what you want it to be." Napoleon Hill, *Think and Grow Rich*

STEP TWO. ACCEPTANCE

"Here's the key: I'm not going to tell you how to change. People don't change. I want you to trust who you already are, and get to that Zone where you can shut out all the noise, all the negativity and fear and distractions and lies, and achieve whatever you want, in whatever you do."
— *Tim S. Grover, Relentless: From Good to Great to Unstoppable*

Imagine this scenario.

You are working a full time day job to pay the bills and keep you in cake and wine and occasionally fun treats, but there is a fire in your belly to write.

You love reading romance or crime [insert your favourite genres here] and spend hours in front of the TV or in the movie theatre absorbing the storylines and the characters, then spend the night dreaming about that emotional experience, reliving the scenes and coming up with your own stories.

So you start writing those ideas down and slowly the shy characters appear and start talking to you, telling you their lives and what, or more likely who, they need to make them happy.

Soon you are writing in the evenings when the kids are in bed and your loved ones are watching television or playing on the Xbox or snoring.

You are scribbling away in your lunch hour and thinking about your story during business meetings.

You are writing and learning and then writing some more and investing in conferences, and meeting other writers and starting to take things seriously.

Great! You even start a blog and learn how to chat on Facebook and Twitter through a process of trial and error.

Then you submit one of your stories to a publisher or enter your work in a contest or a pitch festival and they love it! They want to publish it! Excellent.

Even better. One of your writer friends helps you format one of your novellas, put together a book cover and in a weekend you have loaded it up onto Amazon and Smashwords and there is your book! Your work is out in the world and available for other people to purchase and enjoy on every major online book platform.

You go out with your pals and celebrate.

Congratulations. YOU are a published author!

There is no feeling like it. All of that hard work has been worth it, readers love your work and the five star reviews are flooding in.

Except. Now you have to write more books.

The first book took you 18 months to write by stealing an hour here and there out of your life.

Surely it will get easier now.

No. It gets harder. Much harder.

Especially if you are self-published.

Because now you are going to have to write faster than you have ever written before and create better books with even more compelling characters and story situations.

If you have signed a contract with a publishing house, you will have agreed deadlines so that they can plan the publication schedule well in advance of your next book being written.

How many books a year do you need to write?

An editor told me when I was offered my first publishing contract, that if a debut author wants to create a brand, then they need to create at least three and preferably four books every year, to help readers recognise their name and look for them in the shops and online.

Four books. And the first took you 18 months to complete.

In the rush and heady excitement of being offered a publishing contract, or deciding to self-publish, you say – *"Of course I can write four books a year, that's no problem at all."*

Six months later you are having problems. Because the hard reality is that you don't have the time to write like you had before.

Those precious few hours a day you used to have to write are eaten up by admin and social media, marketing and promotion, and revisions to the last book.

Then life interrupts with holidays, family commitments, a broken boiler and a new puppy.

And...you are rushing around like a headless chicken trying to fit it all in, and failing.

And that brilliant book proposal that your editor loved?

Now you start writing, the idea doesn't work and you want to slap your heroine, but you know the deadline is fast approaching and you don't want to be late on delivery, so you keep battling on to save something from the mess of a book.

So you are working until late every night, then going to work half dead. Your job suffers. Home life suffers. "Mummy I forgot to tell you that I need a dozen cupcakes for tomorrow. And my sports kit needs washing, and...."

When you do snatch a precious half hour to write, you sit down – and there is nothing.

So you find yourself procrastinating with "research" on the internet or frantically checking your sales figures every hour, rather than facing the gaping void that is the empty page.

Fearful of doing the work and not being as good as the last time.

Fearful that you are – no, we all are, in fact, impostors, and this time we are going to be found out, because we have lost the ability to write.

Fearful that we are letting down our talent.

Fearful that we are letting down the people we love.

What happened to that happy dream of being a published author? You start to feel that the joy has been sucked out of the actual writing.

Stop!

Take a deep breath.

Bottom line. This writing lark is a tough business and is getting tougher. Is it any surprise that we are all frazzled and stressed and fearful?

Time to put on your slightly quirky objective hat and stand back and take a hard look at the mental blocks which are holding you back, so that you can address them head on and defeat them for good, before they can sabotage your career.

If you have not completed the motivation exercise in Step One of this book, I would recommend that you work through the questions so that you have a clear vision of your future end results.

If you have worked through the exercise, you should now understand precisely WHAT you want to achieve and you know WHY you want to achieve that amazing end result.

Now it is time to bring out some power tools to build on the success mindset and break down the psychological barriers which threaten to block your progress.

WHY WE PROCRASTINATE

Procrastination is a form of avoidance behaviour.

We procrastinate when we are forced to make a shift in one or more long held rules and self-beliefs, and our deep seated protection mechanisms start fighting back to keep hold of the status quo.

Procrastination Triggers

There is still a huge amount of misunderstanding about procrastination.

The old myths told us, for example, we are just being lazy, indolent and messing about and not prepared to do the work.

Wrong, very wrong and insultingly wrong.

Hard work is not the problem. In fact I believe that most procrastinators work harder than ever before, to compensate for the time spent in avoidance activities.

What we need to do is to work smarter.

The most important step forward out of this cycle of procrastination and frustration is to first recognize that there is a very good reason for why you are avoiding the work, and it has nothing to do with laziness or sloth.

In fact it is all due to our in-built self-protection mechanisms.

ANXIETY, FEAR AND NEUROBIOLOGY

Procrastination is a coping mechanism to avoid anxiety.

"We say we want one thing, then we do another. We say we want to be successful but we sabotage the job interview. We say we want a product to come to market, but we sandbag the shipping schedule. We say we want to be thin but we eat too much. We say we

want to be smart but we skip class or don't read that book the boss lent us." Seth Godin

The human brain has evolved over millions of years into the complex cognitive powerful supercomputer that allows you to see the markings on the paper or screen that you are reading now, by allowing light to be reflected back into photosensitive cells in the retina, interpret these markings as symbols, translate the symbols into words and then the words into meaning and interpretation.

Oh – and carry out all of those tasks in nanoseconds.

But at the core of every astonishing human brain is a self-protection mechanism which is constantly on the lookout for danger and threats. What's more, it is naturally biased towards negative and worst case outcomes.

One of the key concepts I have learnt from Seth Godin is the definition of the "lizard brain". Oren Klaff calls it the "crocodile brain" and Steve Peters "the inner chimp" or "monkey mind".

*Seth Godin, '**The Lizard Brain,**' – "the voice in the back of our head telling us to back off, be careful, go slow, compromise. The resistance is writer's block and putting jitters and every project that ever shipped late because people couldn't stay on the same page long enough to get something out the door. The resistance grows in strength as we get closer to shipping, as we get closer to an insight, as we get closer to the truth of what we really want. That's because the lizard hates change and achievement and risk."*

Steven Pressfield calls this 'voice in our heads' '***The Resistance***' – the block that we have to push through, each and every day.

These are all different ways to describe the oldest and most primitive part of the human brain which evolved with only one purpose – to protect us from danger and keep us alive.

In evolutionary terms we have three main areas of the brain:

The Reptilian/Lizard/Monkey Brain

The reptilian brain, or archipallium, was formed in the oldest part of our brain, above the brain stem. It is responsible for the basic functions such as breathing, our heart rate, sleep, sex and powerful emotions and needs.

The Limbic System

The limbic brain, or paleopallium, developed around and above the reptilian brain. The limbic brain translates the emotional drives and signals from the reptilian brain and helps us to place a context to our feelings and memories.

The NeoCortex

This has only been with us for about three and a half million years when *Homo Sapiens* developed a large neo-mammalian brain in the cerebral hemispheres. The neocortex is responsible for all of our critical higher functioning, problem solving, self-regulation, attention, empathy and thinking processes.

All three areas of the brain work as a network with information super highways crisscrossing and connecting specialist clusters of neurones.

Within the limbic system, there is a small cluster of neurones called the **amygdala**. It controls how we respond to danger and risk by triggering the sympathetic nervous system to produce high-stress chemicals such as adrenaline and cortisone.

The reaction is called the *fight, freeze or flight* syndrome. Our heart starts racing to pump blood and hormones into the muscles so that we are ready to face the danger, our temperature rises and the rest of our body starts to shut down to pump all of our energy into the survival operating mode. The side-effects include dry mouth, sweaty palms and dilated pupils.

When the danger has passed, the para-sympathetic system kicks in and signals to the body that the emergency is over, we are safe now, and it can return to baseline functioning.

The amygdala and the limbic system were brilliant evolutionary advantages for humans when survival was a day to day struggle against predators and the natural world, and is still working in the background of every one of us, ready to step in to protect us from danger.

More importantly, most of the information that feeds into our brain, passes through the limbic system *first* before it is filtered up to the midbrain and finally the neocortex.

Physiologically that makes perfect sense, because there is so much new information and data coming into the brain every millisecond, that the higher functioning parts of the brain would be overwhelmed if the signals were not filtered in some way.

The challenge is this: The human brain cannot distinguish between a physical danger or threat and an imaginary one.

The moment that we start to become anxious about the deep importance, or the stakes associated with a particular project, our body will react by triggering our response to potential risk and harm.

The lizard brain then takes over and makes us run away, because it is designed to keep us safe.

That's why the lizard brain likes situations where you cannot be blamed/get into trouble/ step out of our comfort zone.

The more we care about our work and life and want it to be the best possible, then the more we fear the horror of something going wrong and come crashing down on top of us, and all of the misery and pain and criticism that ***could*** come with that possible failure.

In other words, our fear of a ***future risk*** or threat of pain triggers our brain to shift into attack mode, as though we were facing a real physical danger.

HOW TO STOP THE LIZARD BRAIN FROM SABOTAGING YOUR SUCCESS

- Identify the root cause of the anxiety
- Reduce the risk associated with the task by creating the best possible future outcome for that activity.

Neil Fiore in his book '*The Now Habit: A Strategic Program for Overcoming Procrastination,*' describes the subject this way: ***"Procrastination is a habit you develop to cope with anxiety about starting or completing a task."***

Let's focus on the one crucial word in that definition: **Anxiety.**

The word ***procrastination*** describes the avoidance tactics your body uses to avoid situation based anxiety.

Intolerance of Uncertainty

The lizard brain hijacks our logic reasoning by overestimating the risk or threat associated with a particular activity and refuses to allow the higher functions of the brain to work out a logical recovery strategy.

It wants safety, stability and predictability, not risky new projects where we simply don't know what the outcome will be.

> *"Your brain doesn't want to talk to strangers. It wants comfort. It wants you to be safe. We have the same genes now that we had 40,000 years ago. Talking to someone outside your tribe might have gotten you killed. Hence, your brain will scream and shout and freeze you and cause you actual physical pain if you want to talk to someone new."* James Altucher

That's why we spend hours agonising about whether to email the submission package to a literary agent or publisher. Perhaps we should select a different font, or carry out more background research. Big decisions about what option to go for suddenly become blown up out of all proportion, because we cannot be certain about what the outcome would be.

INSTANT GRATIFICATION RATHER THAN DELAYED GRATIFICATION

That's why we prefer the instant dopamine hit of a delicious iced donut instead of a thinner body sometime in the future, or spending an hour watching daytime soap operas instead of outlining our own book which could provide a pleasurable experience at an unknown future date.

Instant pleasure now or the promise of future pleasure which you don't know for certain will happen. Which option does that rascal lizard brain automatically go for?

The immediate benefits and emotional satisfaction are given greater priority than a theoretical different state at a future date – because we can get the benefits right now. No uncertainty.

FEAR OF SUCCESS

You cannot be certain how success, as you define it, will lead to benefits, or cause you stress and anxiety.

What would happen if you became wildly successful? Are you concerned that it would change the balance of relationships with those around you?

Or do you fear your own talent?

What if the reaction to your work exceeds your expectations? The literary agent and/or publishers and readers love your writing and you receive glowing reviews and accolades. Brilliant! Except now you are expected to produce more work of at least the same quality if not better, and keep on writing brilliant books which reflect your talent.

Can you do it? Or is it better not to deliver the work and maintain the idea that you are unreliable and best left alone.

For example. Your blog is a massive hit and you have thousands of subscribers waiting for your next fascinating, carefully researched blog post. Every day. Adding one more task to your huge to-do list and taking away from your writing time.

PERFECTIONISM, FEAR OF FAILURE AND SELF-DOUBT

Sometimes the world seems obsessed with perfectionism. Images of fashion models are computer-processed to look thinner, cosmetic surgeons have never been busier, the gyms are packed with men and women who are determined to build muscle and there is a never-ending pressure to lose weight, eat this and do that, if you want to be loved and respected.

Children as young as nine are having tutors every evening and weekend so that they can improve their academic and/or sporting performance.

The lesson is clear. Perfection and winning are everything. Imperfection = a loser.

It is madness. Little wonder that this obsession spills over into our creative projects.

Most writers want to create the best work that they are capable of, and set high quality standards for their work, which is absolutely fine.

Perfectionism on the other hand sets unreasonable or unachievable standards, and has destroyed many writing careers.

Are you scared that the book that took you months to write during, for example, a difficult period in your personal life, will be a huge disappointment and need loads of work so that every word is *"perfect"*?

You have just set an impossible standard for yourself, and the harder you work to make it happen, the more anxious you will become.

LOW SELF-ESTEEM AND SELF-CONFIDENCE

Bottom line? We are scared of making a mess of the story idea or project that holds so much promise, and as a result, we are scared of being rejected because the work is flawed.

If you don't finish and submit your work, then you cannot be criticized for sub-standard results or have your work rejected or ridiculed.

This also applies to editing and rewriting. If you have a draft of a manuscript in a drawer and keep bringing it out and reworking it, then pushing it back inside that drawer again, you need to consider why you are scared to finish the manuscript.

So we leave that piece half-finished and start an exciting fresh new project instead, which is untainted by negative feelings and anxieties.

Working on any new exciting project can be outside of our comfort zone and is bound to cause concern and uncertainty.

For example. You know that you should be creating an author platform but that will mean a website and/or a blog. This will take work to set up and a lot more work to update regularly with interesting content.

What if these fail and you have very few visitors and comments to your blog posts? It will only reconfirm that you are wasting your time and energy.

That only leads to feeling stuck, writer's block and stagnation. You can't go forwards or backwards.

We want to be certain that we have not missed anything that could jeopardise our chance of success – or make us fail.

Imperfection = Failure = Rejection and Ridicule = Loss of Self-Belief and Self-Confidence.

"The procrastinator thinks, *'If I never finish, I can never be judged,'* " Joseph Ferrari, a professor of psychology at DePaul University.

"The chronic procrastinator knows he's presenting a negative image, but he'd rather be perceived negatively for lack of effort than for lack of ability," he says. *"Lack of ability is a stable attribute, but lack of effort is shifting—it means you could do it, you might be able to do it."*

Do you see how this cycle quickly starts to circle around and come back to the beginning again, until you are stuck in a loop?

Avoiding the task becomes the easy option.

We can feel so overwhelmed by the amount of work to do and the complexity of it all, that we cannot make a start – the project seems too big and too hard.

There are so many choices to make, it is bewildering. How could you even know where to start?

It feels safer to take the easy option, do the same thing as we did yesterday and leave the decision until we are feeling more in the mood, or after the holidays or busy times at work, when we have more time.

OVERCOMING PERFECTIONISM AND PROCRASTINATION

HOW TO RE-FRAME THE SELF-DOUBT, REDUCE THE ANXIETY AND TRICK THE LIZARD BRAIN

Risk reframing and risk mitigation techniques.

Take the risk away, without dropping your standards.

This is not about lowering your high standards. *Far from it.*

This is about making a shift in your mindset where your self-worth and self-evaluation is not linked to how well you are measuring up against impossible high standards, which in most cases are self-imposed.

As soon as you catch yourself seeking avoidance activities, and new shiny distractions when you know you should be working on a project, stand back and recognise the symptoms. Analyse why you are putting things off.

STAGE #1

Write down on paper the sequence of events and thoughts and feelings you have when you are hit with a crisis of confidence and cannot make a decision or move forward in some way.

Like it or not, we invest a lot of our self-worth into every project that we work on. When someone gives us a bad review or rejects our work, it chips away at our self-esteem and knocks our confidence.

Procrastination is one way of protecting ourselves from that pain.

Worked Example: Imagine you are building up the courage to send a submission package for your novel to a literary agent.

This is your first full length novel and until now the only people to have read it are your two pals who agreed to be beta-readers.

Suddenly the whole submission process spins into overwhelm and takes over your life.

You had no idea you would feel physically sick with emotional turmoil at the thought that someone else is going to judge this book you have slaved over and cared about for years.

What if it is rejected? What if they ask for a full manuscript? And how long will you have to wait for a reply?

This is driving you crazy! Submitting this book has been on your New Year resolution list for two years running. You have rewritten the text through two NaNoWriMo [National Novel Writing in a Month] sessions, edited the third draft and incorporated the feedback from all of your pals.

The manuscript is as good as it can be. In fact you are sick of looking at it.

Worse. You know the longer you delay, the greater the chance that the market will have moved on. Your teen mermaid romance was hot news last year and it can take up to 18 months for publishers to release a hardback print run. That's a geological era in the book world of today.

You want to live up to your potential but you don't want this pressure and stress.

Because: Your internal self-talk is telling you that you are not good enough and that your work is not ready to be judged by anyone. You need to keep working on it.

"If I don't submit, then I won't be judged. I would rather be called slow and lazy than be rejected."

Because: Your excuses are building up every day. You have read that a writer needs to have an author platform before they can submit to an agent or self-publish, but you don't have a website and only a few followers on social media. This is too hard. Don't bother. In fact, just forget about the whole thing. You were stupid to even think that anyone would want to read your stories anyway.

Which results in: You see yourself as a failure. You berate yourself for giving in too easily and you start being supercritical of everything you do, going over and over the same things in your head every day.

Which results in: You keep putting off your writing because the process is now linked to a false memory of anxiety and stress.

Now it is decision time.

#1. Send the submission to the literary agent *today*, or

#2. Forget about the whole thing and let all of that work and an amazing story stay locked inside your computer or stuffed into a box file.

Write down your sequence of events in this way and start to look for the patterns in what you have recorded and how each piece fits together.

STAGE #2

Worst Case Risk Assessment and Correction Strategies

In his book *Tools of Titans*, author entrepreneur Tim Ferriss goes into depth on a technique that he calls ***Fear Setting***. In the business world this process would be called ***Risk Analysis and Mitigation***.

The basic concept is quite simple.

You identify what it is you are scared of doing, write down all of the worst possible negative outcomes that could happen if you went for it, then, one by one, you take the power away from each of these imaginary negative scenarios by describing how you can reduce the impact of that possible outcome and get back to baseline again.

Select one project that you have been putting off.

Take a pad of [preferably ruled] paper and draw two lines down the page so that it is divided into three columns.

1. **In the first column, write down all of the very worst things that could happen if this project fails.**

    Describe these nightmares in great detail. What are your worst doubts and fears about this project?

    Then give each of these possible outcomes a score from 1 to 10, based on whether that negative outcome would have permanent impact, where a score of 1 means no permanent impact, and a score of 10 being permanently life changing.

    For example, leaving your well paid job to write full time when you have not written anything yet, and you have a mortgage to pay every month, might score a 10, while submitting a short story to a magazine could score a 2.

2. **In the second column, write down the very best outcomes if this project is a success.**

    What are the positive outcomes and benefits of this project? These could be internal (such as increased self-confidence and knowledge) or external, such as increased income and better lifestyle.

3. **In the third column, write down how you would recover from each of these negative scenarios that you wrote in the first column if they were to occur.**

    How could you repair the damage and get things back under control?

    What steps would be needed to limit and mitigate the impact of each of those worst case outcomes, and prevent them from happening?

    Don't forget to consider what it would cost you to postpone this action.

    If you don't work on this project, make the phone call or keep the manuscript in the drawer, what will the impact on your life six months, a year or five years from now? There is an opportunity cost associated with inaction and you should write that cost down as part of the risk assessment.

One of the advantages of this technique is that you have to write down all of your fears and concerns on paper.

This gets them out of your head, where they tend to circulate on continuous replay and onto the page where you take a long hard look at them in black and white. In many cases you will see immediately that the fear is not actually valid, or the risk is small compared with the potential benefits that this action could bring to your life.

"Typically, people don't overcome their fears because the fears are nebulous and undefined", Ferriss tells Business Insider. *"To get over them, then, you need to drag your fears out into the open and confront them."*

The fear of an unknown outcome can be very insidious.

By defining the worst case and analysing the possible impact, you can accept that this is a possibility and then identify ways to manage that outcome if it happens.

I have found this is one of the quickest and easiest ways to break through limiting beliefs and mental blocks about a decision or project.

The power of mitigating risk analysis lies in the fact that for most of us, the fear of the unknown is the main reason we are putting things off.

By writing down all of these fears and getting them out of our heads and onto paper, we are taking the emotion out of the imaginary worst case outcome and turning it into a challenge which needs to be addressed and evaluated. In the process we are taking the power away from the lizard brain!

"You come away from that exercise realizing, 'Wow, I was getting extremely anxious and all worked up over something that is completely preventable, reversible, or just not a very big deal," Tim Ferriss.

STAGE #3

Break down each of the activities that you are struggling with into small steps

Here is a psychological trick which releases the stress from the situation and turns it into a learning experience.

Imagine you were telling a friend how to carry out the task you are struggling with, and showing them what to do as a demonstration.

Ask yourself a series of questions – then answer them.

You can answer out loud, or simply write a list of micro-steps down on paper.

Worked Example – how to submit a manuscript to a literary agent

Question #1. If I was going to write a submission letter to an agent, where would I start? What would be the first thing I would do?

Answer #1. Oh, I would check the submission guidelines on their website and make sure that I understand what I have to do to submit the proposal for my book. It only takes a few minutes and we could do it now.

Question#2. Just as an experiment, what is the next thing I would have to do?

Answer#2. I would definitely check I have the correct name and address of the agent that I have been researching for my book. She is a perfect fit and I would love to have her represent my work. The contact details are on the website.

Question#3. Okay, now I have the submission guidelines and the details about the agent, what is the next thing I should do with my manuscript?

Answer#3. Well I would work on a great pitch letter. I even created a draft layout of everything I would write.

Question#4. How can I summarise my book in one paragraph? Have you any tips for a great first line?

Answer#4. I worked on my letter last month but I put it to one side. It's already written and I can show it to you if you like and we can edit it together.

You can see where this is going.

Breaking the traumatic big scary task down into tiny steps takes the emotional drama out of the action and you feel a sense of achievement when you complete each step.

Each tiny step acts as a fractal, a piece of the overall puzzle that will combine with the others to create a complete whole.

The amazing thing is, once you get started, your whole perception of the task and what you are capable of achieving, will be transformed.

Long term goals are like high mountains – huge intimidating structures in the distance, which you can only stare at in terrified awe.

Breaking the task into mini-tasks makes that end result feel solid and achievable.

When you finish each part, the momentum builds with your confidence.

I am not suggesting we all invent imaginary friends, but writing the process down in a sequence like this tricks the brain into thinking that we are not taking a risk, it is simply a demonstration of the process.

You don't have to wait to create your success – you are making the future happen today.

SELF-AWARENESS AND INTERNAL NARRATIVES

We are all uniquely flawed and talented human beings.

This is brilliant in one way. Just think how boring it would be if we were all the same.

The flip side of that is we carry with us the psychological baggage of decades of certain patterns of thinking and belief systems.

Every one of us is a Product of the Stories that we tell Ourselves

Most of those stories are everyday tales of the exciting things we noticed in the supermarket or on the way to work or retelling the headlines in the news.

They create patterns of meaning out of the chaos of the world around us and bring order and sense to events and situations.

Some other stories are more insidious.

These are the stories we make up inside our heads to cope with life, which we use as a type of window, through which we view our lives and our interactions with those around us.

Stories from the past

We all remember some magical moment from a summer holiday or the Christmas mornings and birthday celebrations we had as a child.

If you were going to describe a special childhood beach holiday to someone, which parts of those memories would you include in the story? They would definitely want to hear about the amazing sandcastles you built, swimming in the warm sea with your family and camping outside under the stars.

What about the car sickness, sunburn, family arguments and mosquito bites?

You might want to leave those bits out of the story.

In the same way, if someone asked you to write a biography and describe how you became a writer, there is strong chance that you would pick and choose events from your past and put them together to create a story about how you developed your passion and drive in your topic.

This story would conveniently miss out the negative aspects such as your academic failure, or your total lack of interest in anything to do with work until dire necessity, poverty or threats about deadlines drove you to it.

If you look at press releases from celebrities or business leaders, they often include *one challenge* they had to overcome on the way to their success.

They select *one negative aspect* from their past and then use that event or struggle to contrast where they are now and how far they have come.

It could be anything from poverty, injury, illness, dyslexia, self-abuse, addiction and homelessness to bullying and physical abuse.

We all love to hear an heroic tale about someone who has achieved success despite the odds stacked against them.

These **Zero to Hero** stories are carefully constructed fables and if they tell them over and over again, that person is not only associated with that history but they come to believe it is the only true version of their past.

They craft and manipulate this story about their past in order to present a very specific picture to the world about how they overcame struggles to achieve their current success.

Is it true? Yes, it is probably a one-time event from the past, which, when taken alone would appear to have been a colossal challenge, but is this a selective media or marketing message used to create a "hook"?

For example:

- The former sportsman Lewis Howes. "From his Sister's Couch to 2.5 Million in Revenue Last Year."

- Oprah Winfrey was raised by a single teenage mother and is now an Oscar-nominated actress, a billionaire, and philanthropist.
- J.K. Rowling submitted the manuscript for the Harry Potter to 12 publishers before it was accepted and had very little money to support herself and her daughter at the time. Thanks to the huge worldwide success of the franchise, Rowling is now one of the richest people in Britain.

Are these events the only reason they are successful?

Of course not.

But good luck, relentless hard work, a punishing drive to succeed and meeting the right people at the right time in the right place don't make good sound bites for TV interviews or press releases.

It makes sense for someone building a brand to focus on one simple backstory that they want people to believe and keep on telling the same story to everyone they meet. It is their public identity.

Well guess what? We are all doing precisely the same thing every single day.

We are telling ourselves stories about our past and our future potential which are repeated so many times that they become part of who we and who we will become.

If you grew up in a family where your parents kept telling you that you are too stupid to learn any kind of musical instrument or sports, or that you came from a family of losers and you had better get used to it; that low self-worth, lack of confidence and mistrust will be ingrained into our belief system and can define who we are and what we do today.

Have you ever told a story about an event in your past, and then stopped and thought for a second about whether you can trust your memory about that event?

Did you win the school trophy for tennis or was that your brother?

Did your mother ever tell you out loud that you had to earn her love with good exam grades and doing what you were told, or was that something you believe is true?

HOW TO RE-WRITE THE STORIES WE TELL OURSELVES

If we accept that the most of our fears are based on the unknown future reaction to our work, whether that be fear of rejection, fear of failure, fear of loss or even fear of success, then we can deal with the root cause of the problem.

We can take control of what the future will be like.

We can replace uncertainty with certainty, and substitute worst case predictions of the future with best case predictions.

Start by stepping back from the problems at hand and start working today to shape the future you want for yourself.

#1. What will your future self look like?

Take pen and paper and describe in great detail what your future self will look like when you achieve the final destination for your projects, where and how you shall live and how you will spend each day.

Collect images from magazines or create online photo collages on Pinterest if this helps. By the end of this exercise you will have created a pseudo-memory which is not only motivating but inspiring. *Give yourself permission to believe in this future.*

#2. Sell yourself on your new identity.

Believe this is not only possible but it is going to happen, and it is completely within your personal power to make it happen.

Tell yourself a mini-story about how you came to create this success in your life. Be creative. Create your zero to hero story as though you were chatting to a journalist about your success.

Make up a backstory. Believe in it. Create a memory to replace the old narrative.

Give yourself permission to believe in this new identity.

#3. Create certainty by using hard facts and numbers.

Decide on how you are going to measure progress towards your end results.

Many authors track the wordcount or the number of pages in the current work in progress every day and every week, but the metrics you select are entirely up to you.

Don't waste time with fancy apps and software. A simple chart on a sheet of paper, whiteboard or spreadsheet will work just the same.

Break the project down into bite size chunks and work steadily through them step by step. If life interferes, simply move onto the next section when you are able. Keep moving forward every day towards the end result.

Create a small win every day so that you can tell yourself:

Here is the proof that I can do this.

No more self-doubt. I've got this!

I have all of the tools and skills I need and I will make this project happen.

Give yourself permission to have small wins every day which you can measure and track.

#4. Accept you cannot control the opinion of other people.

You cannot control how other people will react to your work – but you can control how you respond to their feedback.

There are going to be situations where you are working with other people and asking them for their comments on your work. This could be a book proposal to a literary agent, or a draft manuscript to an editor or beta-reader, or a published book released into the wild, fully exposed to anyone who wants to leave an online review.

As a published author, I know what it feels like to have a revision letter from an editor which challenges my story.

The only way to deal with it is by giving the comment or criticism distance. Put any feedback aside for at least 24hrs and then come back, break the comments into chunks and try to be as objective as you can be with your own work. Put yourself into their shoes. You may not agree on every point but you will probably find merit in some, if not all, of their suggestions.

Ask yourself this question: **Is there anything I can say to this person which would make them change their mind?**

If the answer is no, then you would be wasting your precious time coming up with a suitable response.

If you have to reply to the feedback, make it as professional, polite and unemotional as possible. Yes, I know that is hard, but the last thing you want to do is to shift into self-defence or argumentative mood.

You think that you are defending your work and, in turn, yourself, but actually all you are doing is handing over all of the power to the person giving you feedback.

Take a look at some of the social media rants or book reviews on Goodreads or Amazon to see how very damaging public spats can be.

Your new internal narrative says that I respect this person's opinion and I value their feedback. It is not personal. It is simply an opinion.

Give yourself permission to accept that you have no control of other people.

#5. Take complete control of the quality of your work

You may not be able to control the opinions of other people, but you can control how you work and the quality of the work you produce. Nobody will ever be able to say you did not work hard enough to take this project to completion to the best of your ability.

I've got this. Leave it to me to get the job done.

Give yourself permission to take complete ownership for your work.

LEAN INTO YOUR STRENGTHS

Consider this idea.

You already hold within you the **superpower** which is going to provide the fuel for your success.

"The superheroes you have in mind (idols, icons, titans, billionaire, etc.) are nearly all walking flaws who've maximised one or two strengths. Humans are imperfect creatures. You don't succeed because you have no weaknesses; you succeed because you find your unique strengths and focus on developing habits around them." Tim Ferriss.

Your superpower is the strengths and abilities you already possess that make you feel most alive and excited.

"Society's relentless focus on people's shortcomings has turned into a global obsession. What's more, we have discovered that people have several times more potential for growth when they invest energy in developing their strengths instead of correcting their deficiencies." Tom Rath

Let's focus on that last sentence.

What would happen if you focused on what you did best in life, instead of constantly adding to the list of skills and techniques you felt you had to learn before you could become a success in your niche?

Every single one of us has a combination of unique abilities.

We all have things that we do well, and things that we do not do so well.

That is completely normal.

The challenge is that, for most of our lives, we have been taught that we have to find ways to make up for our shortcomings. So we study to pass mathematics or English examinations at school, for example, when actually we are naturally athletic and love to study science and human biology.

The media presentation of a hero or icon is someone who has spent thousands of hours learning a new skill so they can succeed in a particular sport or business. Overcoming weaknesses, lack of natural ability or challenges is seen as something to be applauded and celebrated.

We have all heard the expression – *"You can be anything you want to be, if you just try hard enough"*.

Is that actually true? Or the guaranteed way to make any child, or adult, feel totally inadequate?

When you were at school, did your parents and teachers praise you for your amazing great grades in the subjects which you naturally enjoyed and did well in, or shake their heads at the lowest grades and demand that you work harder and focus on those weak areas so that the grades would improve?

The truth is the exact opposite.

For the majority of people, the key to their success will be to develop, practise and work hard on those innate skills and talents that they already possess, when they feel invigorated and engaged and excited about what they are doing.

Focusing on your natural authentic talents, means your work will be aligned to your true potential and you will achieve much greater returns for your hard work and practice. You will be building on your strengths which in turn will become your most powerful assets.

READY TO START UNCOVERING YOUR STRENGTHS?

Begin by answering these ten questions:

Question 1. If you won the lottery tomorrow and had the freedom to spend your time and money doing something you would love to do more of, what would that be?

Would you go back to university for example, or spend more time travelling to research a topic you feel passionately about? Would you take yourself off on a writing retreat in a fabulous location for a month? Go wild! You can go anywhere and do whatsoever you want.

Give yourself permission to retune your energy and emotional power back to those things which truly delight you.

Question 2. What do people tell you that you are good at? What do you receive compliments about?

This could be soft skills such as empathy, listening and caring, as well as technical and business skills such as computer coding, proofreading, copyediting and interior design. If you enjoy volunteering in the community, what aspects are you drawn to?

Give yourself permission to ask those friends or family members who know you best what they feel are your special gifts.

Question 3. What hobbies or interests do you spend time doing now, or have done in the past, that you enjoy so much that you lose all track of time?

If you have a spare hour to spend on your own each day, how would you spend that free time in total self-indulgence? These are the tasks you would instinctively do because they energise and engage you and you love to spend time in that zone.

Give yourself permission to allocate time in your diary to develop those hobbies or interests so that you can master them

Question 4. What skill or talent comes so naturally to you that you don't even have to think about it, but other people struggle with?

What topic could you talk about for hours off the cuff, without looking at a single script?

For example, not everyone can run marathons, bake bread, sew their own clothes, write short stories, research military tactics and create spreadsheets and slide decks.

Give yourself permission to take pride in your talent and skill.

Question 5. If someone asked you what you were good at, how would you answer?

Your reply might include something you are proud of achieving in your life, from climbing Mount Everest to being a single parent to teenagers, or a skill you have developed over the years, such as oil painting, making silver jewellery or website coding.

When you carry out those tasks you feel comfortable and know that you are in control of the work.

Give yourself permission to step up and reply with a list of skills and strengths that make you happy, which might have nothing to do with your academic qualifications.

Question 6. Do you feel you work better on your own, or do you love the buzz that comes with being part of a much larger team?

Give yourself permission to accept your strengths lie in a particular way of working.

Question 7. Do you feel that you have any skills and abilities you have pushed to one side because of your other life choices?

Think back to when you were 9 years old, then 15. Can you remember what you were obsessively interested in? What did you love to do?

Give yourself permission to look back and recall a time in your life when you instinctively knew that you were good at something and enjoyed it and wanted to learn more.

APPLYING YOUR STRENGTHS

Now take a moment to read through your answers and spot any common themes that might emerge.

Where and when do you feel most engaged and enthusiastic and energised about what you are doing?

Are you best working on your own or do you really enjoy teamwork and the fast paced feedback from people around you?

What kind of projects would make best use of your innate skills and talents so that they seem effortless and yet totally rewarding? Then think about your projects.

Do you prefer longer research based projects such as extensive craft projects or writing non-fiction books, courses and educational materials, where you can learn intricate detail about your topic, or short projects you can complete in the fastest time possible.

Working on projects where you can make best use of your skills and talents will be the fastest way forwards for a rewarding and fulfilling career.

How to Deal with your Weaker Areas as a Creative Entrepreneur

Now that you have recognised and honed in on your natural potential and passions there are bound to be areas of your ideal business project where you are not going to have the talent or skillset to excel.

This is part of the acceptance process.

It is all too easy to use this as an excuse to feed your negative self-talk and self-doubt.

Instead, the strategic approach is to stay positive and recognise and accept that you may not excel in every aspect of your project, and you will have to take action to correct that deficit.

There are three options.

Option One. You don't do anything and decide to spend all of your energy on your strengths and superpower.

I know several fiction authors who want to focus on their superpowers, creating compelling fiction, and would rather eat their own feet than learn how to market and promote their work. They don't have any social media or other kind of platform and refuse to do so. Their work is sold and distributed by their publisher without any involvement from the author.

These authors recognise and accept that marketing their author branding is not an area they want to spend time on and have made the informed decision not to do so.

Option Two. You use the Pareto 80/20 Principle and learn just enough about the gap in your knowledge to achieve an effective level of results which gets the job done.

This can be the best way to maximise your time so you can focus on your talent. The trade-off is that this aspect may not be perfect, but it works.

For example, as a fiction author, I recognise that my strengths and talents include characterisation and story structure. I am not naturally gifted at website design, but I know I want to build an author platform which includes an author website. That's why I decided to go for a simple self-hosted Wordpress website using a free theme that they provided. I can update pages and blog posts in minutes. No fuss. No time wasting.

I am not an expert but I can follow the video tutorials and instructions to achieve a website which works well and is easy to maintain.

Other authors have learnt how to do Facebook advertising and how to self-publish their work on the online publishing platforms using free online tutorials.

Option Three. You delegate those skills and pay someone who is an expert to do the work for you.

Which parts of your project you select to outsource to freelancers or experts will depend on the type of project you are working on, but the objective should always be to recoup your investment as quickly as possible.

For example. Many authors who self-publish their work, including myself, pay for editors to review their manuscript and professional cover design for their book. These investments not only cut out months of the learning cycle but the quality of the final result will be better.

These are legitimate business expenses for services which will help your work to stand out from the crowd, and deliver a great experience for the reader.

"One thing to keep in mind... is that the most successful people don't take on everything themselves. They focus on their strengths and delegate their weaknesses to specialists. Some authors try to do too much themselves and end up shooting themselves in the foot because they end up with a weak link." Derek Doepker

Productivity, put simply, is the name that we give our attempts to figure out the best uses of our energy, intellect, and time as we try to seize most meaningful rewards with the least wasted effort.

It is a process of learning how to succeed with less stress and struggle. It's about getting things done without sacrificing everything we care about along the way.

Productivity isn't about working more or sweating harder. It's not simply a product of spending longer hours at your desk or making bigger sacrifices.

Rather, productivity is about making certain choices in certain ways. The way we choose to see ourselves and frame daily decisions; the stories we tell ourselves, and the easy goals we ignore.

"Amplify your strengths rather than fix your weaknesses. The point is thinking about, 'What is the unique mojo that I can bring, and how can I try and amplify that?'" Chase Jarvis. Tools of Titans.

MINDSET SHIFT: RESULTS ORIENTATED LIVING

The business entrepreneur Scott Oldford describes having a meeting with Scorpion, the Irish born billionaire who is one of the top five in the world in terms of IQ, who even has a popular television show that is based on his mission.

Scorpion became a billionaire, not by thinking big, but by:

- **Identifying the specific end result that he wanted to achieve.**
- **Deciding to do what it takes to make it happen.**

Once that decision was made, then all of his actions, in everything he did, were aligned to creating that exact final result.

GROWTH MINDSET >> POSITIVE SELF-TALK >> RESULTS ORIENTATED ACTION

Results oriented living allows you to focus on what is most important to you, and actually makes your life very much easier, since the decision making process is centred on that final result.

In step three of this book we will work through project planning and how to use the gap analysis technique to create the ideal, simple, sequence of steps which will take you from where you are now to where you want to be.

This will form the basis of a game plan designed to make your power list projects into reality.

"Success in writing—and by that, I mean getting the contents of your head out onto the page in a form that other people can relate to—is largely a matter of playing mind games with yourself. In order to get anywhere, you need to figure out how your own mind works—and believe me, people are not all wired up the same way."
Diana Gabaldon

"HOPE IS NOT A STRATEGY, LUCK IS NOT A FACTOR, FEAR IS NOT AN OPTION." Tee-shirt logo from the movie Avatar created by James Cameron.

Summary of Key Learning Points from Step Two: Acceptance.

Let's quickly recap the important points from this chapter.

Acceptance. You have acknowledged and accepted your unique strengths and limitations and know that resistance will be part of your journey but you still want to continue.

- Why we Procrastinate
- Anxiety, Fear and Neurobiology
- Self-Awareness and Internal Narratives
- Self-Belief and Self-Image. Leveraging the power of self-motivation
- Self-Doubt and Perfectionism. Risk reframing techniques.
- Lean in to your Strengths

BONUS CONTENT

Go to http://ninaharrington.com/Bonuses to Download a Free Copy of a Chapter Extract: Overcoming Perfectionism and Procrastination

STEP THREE. GAP ANALYSIS

"If you don't go after what you want, you'll never have it. If you don't ask, the answer is always no. If you don't step forward, you'll always be in the same place." Nora Roberts

Why a Gap Analysis Is So Valuable

A gap analysis will help you to:

- Put a marker in the sand for precisely what your end destination will look like and how you will recognise it when you get there.
- Define the metrics you can use to measure your progress, as you complete each step on the way.
- Break down the big chunks of work into smaller and smaller pieces so that you can see how you can take action in the most effective way possible.
- Work out the fastest way from the starting point to your final destination.
- Break free of the "let's see what happens" mentality.
- Take ownership for the project plan.

THE THREE CORE QUESTIONS THAT MAKE UP ANY GAP ANALYSIS

#1. Where are you now as regards this project?

#2. What is your final dream destination? Can you describe it in detail?

#3. What is the gap between where you are now and where you want to go?

In Step One we talked about why you need to have both crystal clear motivation and a success mindset to reach a final destination for your unique journey as an author entrepreneur.

This journey will be made up of individual projects which act as stopping places on the road to where you want to go.

A career author does not write one book, but an entire portfolio of work. Novels, short stories, articles and blog posts all combine to build into a body of professional fiction, or non-fiction writing.

Each one of those projects takes you one step forward on the path to the end result that you seek to achieve.

Some people like to describe this final objective as an end goal, but for me this is not just a single goal which can be measured by one discrete metric, such as having a book in the New York Times Bestseller list, or winning a literary prize.

Reaching the final destination is a lot more than that.

It is the culmination of your powerful vision for your future identity and lifestyle.

Whatever your deep motivation, there is a world of difference between yearning to achieve a certain end result and taking specific and targeted steps to make it happen.

GOALS VERSUS END RESULTS.

In his bestselling book ***The Code of the Extraordinary Mind,*** author Vishen Lakhiani challenges us all to create new rules for our lives so we can define success on our own terms.

One of the most important concepts to grasp is the idea that there are two kinds of goals:

Means Goals. They are the specific steps we take to achieve a particular objective. For example: if you wanted to write the first draft of a 50,000 word novel, you could set yourself a goal of writing 5,000 words a week for ten weeks. The goals are the means we take to reach a target.

End goals are typically feeling orientated and tend to fall into three categories:

- human experiences,
- human growth, self-actualisation and self-fulfilment
- contribution to your community and how you can leave a legacy in the world.

Most people set themselves means goals – but they actually want end goals, which are linked to their happiness.

Think about the deep reasons why you want to write your book. What do you *really* want to achieve?

What would you do with your life if money was not an issue and you had complete freedom to live how and where you wanted?

For example: Is your objective is to write and publish a book, share your story and see your name on the cover?

Or is this book only one part of a much larger end goal?

For example: Many authors want to build a creative home based business so that they can spend more time with their children and other loved ones, while generating an income. Writing is their way of escaping from being an employee, realising their creative potential and enabling a completely flexible lifestyle.

Once you know what you truly want in life as a writer, you can start to work on building a strategic plan to achieve that vision for the future, focused on end goals which are linked to your happiness.

What experiences do you want to have, both now and in the future?

One of the most effective ways to kick start that process, is by carrying out a gap analysis.

HOW TO LEVERAGE THE POWER OF A GAP ANALYSIS

Way too many creative entrepreneurs simply dive into the work, raring to go, once they have their true "fire in the belly" list of one or more projects that they cannot wait to start work on.

They are frightened that they will lose the momentum and energy of the excitement and enthusiasm that comes with having deeply motivated dreams for an amazing future destination.

This is completely understandable, but it can be a big mistake.

Working on the **right things** but in the **wrong order** can not only waste time, energy and money but throw you off track when you have to go back and forth, and fill in the gaps you should have done the first time around.

It is definitely worth spending an hour of your time with a pad of paper, or a spreadsheet if you are scientifically inclined [puts hand up], to work out exactly *how* you are going to move from where you are now to where you want to be.

Have you ever heard the old joke about: *How Do You Eat An Elephant?* The answer is not, you start at the trunk or at the tail, but: *One Piece at a Time.*

Same thing here.

I know that some creatives don't like looking at the big picture because it can be intimidating and overwhelming to see how much work you need to do to reach that final dream destination.

Don't be scared.

This is not intended to frighten you off from starting in the first place.

In fact a gap analysis can be one of the most motivating things that you can do for any project, creative or otherwise. It is a powerful way of transforming a nebulous idea or vision into concrete action steps which bring the project to life. Suddenly you can see that your vision is achievable, and a lot closer than you had imagined.

HOW TO USE A GAP ANALYSIS AS THE GPS FOR YOUR PROJECT PLAN

The basic principle is that you work backwards from the end destination and plan your journey as a logical sequence of steps, which will take you all the way down to where you are now.

By "reverse engineering" your project, you can create a simple one-page plan of all the key stages. Then you break down each stage into smaller actions steps.

Note: In a top level gap analysis, you don't think about how you are going to make this happen or when or where. You are simply writing out a road map of the key steps and stages on the journey to reach your end destination in the most effective way possible.

Think of it as though you were planning a road trip or adventure holiday.

A map of the main route can be super handy to have in your hand before you set out!

Yes – of course you will find interesting diversions and side roads along the way that you might want to visit, but the main highway has to be clearly marked, otherwise you could find yourself wandering in the woods for hours or even days, without a landmark in sight to guide you back on track.

Your gap analysis is your GPS of the route you want to take to complete the project.

You can carry out a gap analysis at a high level on the overall plan that you have, and then repeat the process for each individual project you would need to complete within the plan.

Reminder: THE THREE CORE QUESTIONS

#1. Where are you now as regards this project?

#2. What is your final dream destination? Can you describe it in detail?

#3. What is the gap between where you are now and where you want to go?

The best way to demonstrate the power of this technique is by using case studies with practical examples.

WORKED EXAMPLE ONE; A FICTION AUTHOR WHO WANTS TO CHANGE GENRE

There are many fiction authors who write in more than one genre. They have different pen names and writing personas so that readers are not confused.

J.K.Rowling, for example, writes teen fantasy books, but as Robert Galbraith, she is free to explore crime and literary fiction.

What would happen if you currently wrote paranormal erotic romance and had a brilliant idea for a middle grade fantasy that your teenage children would love to read?

#1.Where you are now? You have an idea for a major series of teen fantasy novels, but have not written a book in this genre and don't have any experience in the teen market. You *believe* you would love to write these books, but are not quite sure yet.

#2.What is your fantasy final destination? The complete series of teen novels in print and for sale in a bookstore, plus electronic and audio formats, film rights sold and the story ideas worked into comic books and games.

#3.What is the gap between where you are now and where you want to go?

This is where you write down as many steps that you can think of, as quickly as you can.

You know that to get started, you would need to:

- Complete the first book in the series as an experiment.
- Test whether you enjoy writing in this new genre.
- Create an author platform and start building a brand for your teen fiction with a new pen name. This would include purchasing a new domain name, building a new website and creating social media platforms for your new brand identity.
- Build new connections with authors in this genre.
- Learn more about the craft of writing teen fantasy fiction. Books, movies, training courses and professional organisations could help.

- Research those publishers who specialise in this genre.
- Research the names of literary agents who accept manuscripts for teen fantasy.
- Submit the first book to the first on your list of specialist children's literary agents.
- Work with your dream publisher to print and release the first book of a series.
- [And much more you have not considered yet.]

The scale of this new initiative is quite daunting, but the entire sequence kicks off with that crucial first step; writing and polishing the first book in the series.

Until you write the book and dive deep into the characters and their fantasy story world, you don't know if this is the genre that will dominate the next few years of your life.

The logical next step therefore, is to work on a gap analysis of the first project on the bottom rung of the ladder; creating the first novel in the series.

WORKED EXAMPLE TWO: A TRADITIONALLY PUBLISHED TEEN FANTASY NOVEL.

In your vision for your final destination, you can see your book on the bestseller shelf at your local bookstore. The cover art is precisely how you imagined it, and the title and your name leap out at you from the shelf.

THAT is your final outcome for this book. You want to see your book, in print from a traditional publisher and available for sale in bookstores, plus other formats.

Okay. Now we know what we want.

Let's work backwards from that end point and brainstorm all of the intermediate broad stages between your published book and your story idea.

Product Launch Sequence for a Start-Up Business

1. Idea for a new product.
2. Validation that there is a market for this product.
3. Product design and development, followed by beta-testing.
4. Build the final product.
5. Launch as quickly as possible.
6. Refine the product after customer feedback.
7. Relaunch version two or second product in a series.

Applying the Start-Up Business Mentality to Writing

The key thing to remember is that you are working strategically and thinking about the business aspects of what you are going to write, as well as the creative and craft elements.

For Example: Imagine that you are a fiction writer

- You have a great idea for a teen fantasy novel.
- You carry out extensive research by using the bestseller charts and online book stores to assess the current market for teen fantasy novels similar to the storyline that you would like to write.
- Is there an audience who would pay for your story?
- Armed with the hard data that there is a market for your teen fantasy story idea, you work on the outline and write the opening chapters of the book.

- Then you test your idea is strong enough by sending your submission package to literary agents who specialise in this genre, and/or to readers who are passionate about the genre.
- Following feedback, you complete the entire manuscript and revise and polish it.
- You send the manuscript to the literary agent or beta-readers.
- You get the feedback and edit the book.
- You submit the final version of the manuscript to a literary agent or self-publish the novel depending on the publishing model that you have chosen for this book.

As you are working on your manuscript you should be spending time every day to work on "the business" aspects of a platform for your author brand in the niche that you want to write in.

If you have been building an email list of readers who love this genre, for example, through regular promotions and giveaways and great content, then these readers can become your first customers when your book launches.

#1.Where are you now? An idea for a teen fantasy novel.

#2.What is your final destination? That novel in print and for sale in a bookstore.

#3.What is the gap between where you are now and where you want to go? Right now the gap is the entire creation and publishing sequence, since you have not taken the first on the journey from an idea for the book, to a printed book on sale in a bookstore.

A Typical Publication Sequence for the Traditional Publishing Route for a Teen Fantasy Novel

Stage#10. Book published by traditional publishing house and distributed to bookstores.

Because...

Stage#9. Book accepted by an editor at a publishing house after submission from a literary agent who specialises in teen fantasy fiction.

Because...

Stage#8. Manuscript accepted by a literary agent who agrees to represent you.

....

Because...

Stage#7. Manuscript submitted to a literary agent who accepts teen fantasy fiction.

Because...

Stage#6. Research list completed of literary agents in your country who specialise in that genre of teen children's books.

Because...

Stage#5. Manuscript completed, edited and proofread. Your third draft is a polished novel which is ready to submit it to a literary agent.

Because...

Stage#4. Second draft of manuscript self-edited.

Because...

Stage#3. Second draft of manuscript completed and ready to be edited.

Because...

Stage#2. Your outline of the story idea has been transformed into a working first draft of the manuscript.

Because...

Stage#1. You have created a working outline of the key story points of your novel based on your original story idea.

Of course this is a very simplified breakdown of the main stages, but you get the idea.

In this gap analysis there are ten stages to cover on the journey between your story idea and your published book in a bookstore.

You will note that I have added a dotted line after stage #7, when you have submitted your manuscript to a literary agent. This line indicates a cut-off point.

From stages one to seven, you are in control and driving the action.

From stage #8 the timeline for this example is being driven and controlled by other people.

You don't know how long it will take to attract your ideal literary agent and go through the process of being represented to publishing editors, who, in turn, can take months to come back with an offer or who could ask for revisions prior to considering the book.

Those are the unknown factors in the sequence.

You *can* control how and when you write, and polish, the best book that you are capable of, so that it has a chance of being accepted by a literary agent.

Now you know the overall road map, you can get to work on the next level of planning for each stage.

At this point there are two key questions which you need to answer:

- **Following on from the last section on acceptance, how much time and energy can you allocate to this project every week?**

- **Do you have a realistic estimate of how much time each stage of the project plan needs to complete? And therefore how long do you need to work on the project before you see the final results?**

Using Wordcount as a Metric

At this point it is useful to select ONE metric which you can use to measure your progress in the project.

Most writers make a note of their daily and weekly wordcount to track the development of a manuscript.

Simply record the computer word count of your document each day in your diary, chart or spreadsheet, and keep a running tally.

It you write by hand, you can record the number of pages you complete in each session.

It is easy to do and very motivating!

Let's use Worked Example Two: A Traditionally published Teen Fantasy Novel, and work through and expand on these questions.

Question One. How much time and energy can you allocate to this project every week?

Your personal circumstances are unique to you and your gap analysis has to reflect that.

We all have to react to the daily challenges and emergencies which manage to suck away most or all of the time allocated to long term proactive projects such as your writing.

Time and Energy Audit.

It is crucial that you are totally honest with yourself about how much time and energy you have in your life for creative work. It is not much use writing 3,000 words when you are exhausted and frazzled by distractions and then deleting 2,000 of them the next day.

School holidays and family and personal commitments are a precious part of your family and social life, and you have to include them into any calculation of your available time.

Your writing goals have to be built into an overall and realistic plan so your physical and mental health are protected, your family and friends are still priorities in your life, and you stay sharp and creative.

The alternative is to burn yourself out which leads to frustration, disappointment and self-flagellation and ... giving up.

It is far better to carry out an audit of your available time and energy now and be honest with yourself.

For example; let's say your target word count for your first draft of this teen novel is 80,000 words.

If the only time you have to write is in your lunch break or during the commute to your day job, then an average of 1,000 to 2,000 words a day spread out over the entire week would be an achievable target [about 4 to 8 pages a day]. You could, and probably will, do more but that is a realistic assessment.

This could give you a minimum output of 5,000 "keeper" words every week. You decide how many days you want to work each week and what you can squeeze into the days available.

On the other hand, if you are able to steal several hours a day to write, then your daily word count could be 2,000 to 3,000 words, or 10,000 to 15,000 "keeper words" every week.

What are "keeper words"?

This is the text that will make it into your working first draft of your novel. Your notes or scraps of ideas for dialogue are great and super useful, but they probably won't be used in the final manuscript. "Keeper words" is the text you want to share with readers.

If you can manage to write 5,000 words a week, this means that you will need at least 16 weeks to create the first draft of your 80,000 word novel.

If you can write 10,000 words a week, this would fall to 8 weeks.

Question Two. Do you have a realistic estimate of how much time each stage of the project plan needs to complete?

You should have a good idea of how long you need to work on the project before you see the final results.

To answer that question, you need to work backwards from the endpoint, as we have just done, and estimate how long it would take to complete each stage in the process.

Here is an example of a typical ten step timeline for a traditionally published teen fantasy of 80,000 words if you can write around 5,000 words a week.

Stage	Actions Needed to Complete this Stage	Maximum Time You Need to Allocate	Total Time
10	Book published and distributed.	Can be up to 18 months for a print run following revision and acceptance.	Publisher dependent
9	Book accepted by an editor at a publishing house	Can be 3 months or longer for a literary agent to find an editor who loves your work	Up to 6 months in some cases
8	Manuscript accepted by a literary agent	It can take 3 months or longer to hear from your first rounds of agents.	Up to 12 months and many rounds of submissions

From stages one to seven, you are in control and driving the action. From stage 8 the timeline for this example is dependent on other people.

Stage	Actions Needed to Complete this Stage	The Maximum Time You Would Need to Allocate to this Stage	Total Time
7	Manuscript submitted to a literary agent who accepts teen fantasy	At least 2 or 3 days to prepare a synopsis and submission letter.	26 weeks
6	Research list completed of literary agents	2 or 3 days.	25 ½ weeks
5	Manuscript completed, fully edited and proofread	Final structural editing, copy-editing and proof-reading, ideally by Beta-readers, 3 weeks.	25 weeks
4	Editing a second draft of the manuscript	At least 1 week.	22 weeks
3	Second draft of manuscript completed	4 weeks as an example at 5000 words a week.	21 weeks
2	A working first draft of the manuscript	16 weeks as an example at 5000 words a week.	17 weeks
1	A working outline of the book based on your idea	At least 1 week.	1 week

Working the Numbers

If you can write an average of 5,000 words a week [allowing for holidays and other commitments] and can revise your first draft in four weeks, then it should take about 26 weeks, or around six months, to complete the finished, polished manuscript of your 80,000 word novel. At that point it should be ready for submission to a literary agent, or self-publishing if you decide that publishing model is the best option for this book.

Six months? I can't wait six months!

Yes. You can.

If you want to write the novel that has been burning inside of you for years, then this is how long it will take if you can only manage 5000 words a week.

Every novel will demand more of you than your time and energy. A full gap analysis should help you to identify the hidden costs up front. How much is this teen fantasy novel going to cost you to complete?

WHERE DO YOU HAVE TO MAKE A FINANCIAL INVESTMENT?

The Manuscript

This is your career. Your name is on the cover and it is crucial that this book is as fault free as it can be before you even think of asking literary agents [or paying readers, if you are self-publishing] to read it.

The only way around this is to hire an experienced editor who can spot plot holes, suggest changes and copyedit your work. Another pair of eyes will spot errors and omissions that you will not believe that you and your spouse/friends/family missed.

The good news is that the upheaval in the publishing industry has led to many excellent and highly experienced senior editors leaving publishing to work as freelance book consultants.

The bad news is that editing your book will take days of an editor's time for an 80,000 word book, and that costs money.

You have to decide on what kind of editing you need.

a. Story Editing for Fiction Writers. There are some editorial services that can offer story and content development support, where the editor will look at the story structure of the whole manuscript and suggest how you can develop, for example, the character arcs and plot structure to strengthen the novel.

Many authors use friends and 'beta-readers' to provide this service for free in exchange for you doing the same for their book, but you have to make it clear that you want an unbiased opinion, and a strict tough-love approach.

You should expect to pay an editor for a couple of hours of careful reading and note taking to produce an effective and detailed report on your work.

b. Copy Editing. This is what most authors think of when they hire an "editor".

Not all writers are gifted with a strong sense of grammatical structure, and the correct placement of commas and other punctuation is fraught with difficulty. Copy editors, or line editors, are also excellent at recognising words which have the correct spelling but are in completely the wrong place. Writers who use voice recognition software to dictate their work find this a particular problem.

Copy editors tend to charge by the number of words they have to read in your book, or by the number of hours needed, so the longer the book the higher the fee. This is fair and logical.

c. Proofreading. Essential. And often the one thing many authors think that they can do themselves. For this task you need someone who is totally objective, and preferably someone who has never seen this book before.

Every author needs an independent proof-reader, because no matter how many times you go through your manuscript, [I read my books from the back and going forwards] there are bound to be typos and errors that slip through. These glitches will pull the reader out of your book and they may not pick it up again.

You can hire a professional proof-reader or ask another writer who you can trust to be diligent and a perfectionist.

How do you find an editor you can trust?

Use the power of the Internet to research editors who specialise in your kind of work and look at their clients. For example, a quick Internet search picked up, completely at random, over 22,000 websites advertising fiction editorial services and almost 4,000 of these were in the U.K. Editorial services for commercial fiction that I am familiar with in the U.K. include Cornerstones, BubbleCow and RustonHutton.

Word of mouth recommendations from other authors who are writing similar books to your own and used editors in the past.

I used an editor who I had previously worked with in a traditional publishing house, and who I knew would not hesitate to point out how the work could be improved for the reader.

So how much does a freelance editor cost? That depends on their rates and what you ask them to do and how many cycles your book has to go through, but I would suggest having a budget of at least $800 for Story Editing and at least $650 for Copy Editing.

The Society for Editors and Proof Readers has a recommended minimum charge structure, but this is only a guideline.

TIME AND ENERGY COSTS

You are going to have to work hard to transform your revised manuscript into a polished piece of prose, which could have been published by any of the big traditional publishers.

Time is money.

Most authors work on several projects at the same time, so spending extra time and energy on one project means less time on others.

This can be particularly stressful when you have a day job, plus family commitments where your loved ones want to spend time with you.

In that situation, the creative initiative will slip lower and lower down your priority list. But you have already invested too much time and energy and cash in this book to let it fail. You have to keep working on it.

TIME INVESTMENT STRESS

Stress and anxiety are common reasons why authors often abandon their books. It is too much work for an unknown future benefit, and existing commitments have to take priority. There are no guarantees that your book will sell or be accepted by a literary agent who loves it and agrees to represent you.

We have talked more about the power of instant gratification versus delayed benefits in the future in Step Two. The key thing to recall is that you are working slowly on a small step in a larger project.

Make each achievement a small win, and you will build momentum and reinforce the progress that you are making. Even if it does take six months to complete your novel.

BUILDING YOUR PLATFORM

If you have built up a significant social media platform and have published the same type of book in the past, then you know your work will find an audience. You need to plan how to communicate details of your new work and at the same time build your existing platform. Your readers are enormously important and the last thing you want to do is disappoint them.

If you are building a new audience from scratch, then you will need to allocate time in the high level gap analysis to spend on building a platform and connecting to author authors and readers in that niche.

MOTIVATION

Whenever you launch into any new enterprise, you have to expect that there will be ups and downs in your energy, motivation and enthusiasm.

It is quite possible that your beta reader, or a literary agent or editor, comes back to you with a 20 page list of problems, which will mean that you have to go back to the beginning of your manuscript and re-write several sections, or weave in a new story thread or character arc in a novel to make the rest of the story work. This means you have to create a new manuscript, which will need to be edited again.

The high expectations and hopes are going to be quickly dashed by the amount of work you know you are going to have to do, to make this document the best that it can be.

The 'Trough of Disillusionment' is very real, and the more this project matters to you on a personal level, then the deeper that trough can become.

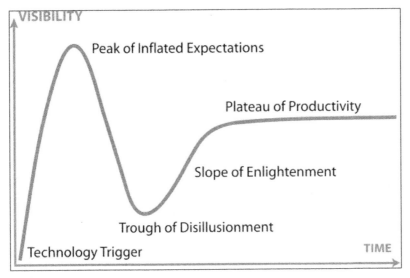

Image Credit: The Gartner Hype Cycle representing the maturity, adoption and social application of specific advances in new technology and ideas.

It's crunch time

At this point you should have:

- **a very clear idea about the gap between your current stage in a project,**
- **what your fantasy end result looks like, and**
- **what it will take to get there and how much resource it will need, and what it will cost.**

You should have all of the facts and data that you need to get started.

Now you have to make an informed decision.

Are you willing to pay the price to make this project happen?

Are you going to start on the bottom rung of this ladder and take the next step on your project?

Or stop now and put it to one side?

If you do not want to commit to this project, then now is the time to realise that the project is not right for you at this time, and back out.

The power of Decision and Self-Determination

The key to making things happen in your life is to stay deeply invested in the **reasons why you are working on this project.**

You are in control of your future.

This is your work and you own it.

No more *"letting things just happen when you feel like it".*

Self-determined entrepreneurs feed on the clarity that we considered in Step One and use it as fuel to drive their motivation every day.

If you haven't read Step One, I would encourage you to go back and work through it now. Your deep internal motivation is unique to you and your circumstances in life, but there is one universal truth that underpins everything that we do.

Once you have taken the decision to start a project and see it through to the end, no matter how long that might take, then you have the power to change your life.

EXERCISE FOR STEP THREE: GAP ANALYSIS

Now it is time for you to create your own timeline for your writing project. Grab a pen and paper and write down the answers to the three critical questions as quickly as you can.

#1.Do you have a realistic outline plan for your project?

Quickly sketch out a sequence of steps as described in the earlier worked example, starting with the completed project and working backwards to where you are now. Don't be scared to think big!

Break the entire sequence of events down into small chunks and stages which you can measure. It could take a lot more than ten steps.

#2.How much time and energy can you allocate to this project every day and every week?

One hour a day? Two hours a day? It does not have to be one continuous block of time. Many authors, including myself, write in 20 or 30 minute timed sessions.

Can you block out two 30 minute sprints every day for five days a week? Or can you manage more than that?

Be brutally honest. If you can work effectively for an hour a day, even if that hour is broken into three separate 20 minute timed writing sessions, that is a brilliant achievement and you will make progress.

#3. Can you create an achievable timeline for this project based on the answers to questions #1 and #2?

You know how much time you have to work on the project.

Many authors set themselves a target number of words per week to measure progress. Could that work for you?

Using this approach, create a timeline plan for your project for the next six months, and then work backwards to the next three months, and then the next four weeks.

"If you talk about it, it's a dream, if you envision it, it's possible, if you schedule it, it's real." Tony Robbins

BONUS CONTENT
Go to http://ninaharrington.com/Bonuses to Download a Free Copy of the Ten Point Gap Analysis Chart and Question Sheet

STEP FOUR. IMPLEMENTATION

Execution is everything.

"The secret of getting ahead is getting started. The secret of getting started is breaking your complex overwhelming tasks into small manageable tasks, and starting on the first one." Mark Twain

CREATING AN IMPLEMENTATION STRATEGY

Brilliant!

If you have followed the previous chapters, you now have:

- A "fire in the belly" list of power projects which excite you just thinking about them.
- An honest assessment of your strengths and skillset, and the challenges that you face. Self-awareness is super important for any entrepreneur, no matter what business you are running.
- A complete gap analysis of both the overall plan for your final destination as a writer, and an outline plan of what you need to do to complete the first step on the journey.

Now it is time to execute the plan and create a strategy which will make sure that you stay on track towards that end objective, while fitting around your life.

Don't worry, this is not the business plan kind of strategy.

This is the nitty gritty grown up kind of strategy which is honest and open and real, without being scary.

It is simply a sequence of steps which will take you from where you are now, to where you want to go.

One thing is clear. There are 1,440 minutes in every 24 hours.

It is up to us to make best use of those precious minutes in the most effective and enjoyable way possible.

That's why we all need to schedule writing time into a plan.

Strategy Essentials

To build out an effective Implementation Plan you need five things:

- Complete clarity about why you are working on this project, backed up with a technicolour 3-dimensional picture inside your head, or printed out and taped to your wall, of what your ideal end result will look and feel like.

- An honest assessment of where you are now with regard to the first step on the path to your ideal end objective.

- A timeline with a target deadline when you want this project to be complete. You set this out during your gap analysis. Then you need to break down the project into small blocks of sequential activity.

- Write your goal down on paper or a giant sticky note, rather than using an online planning system. This creates clarity in your mind and acts as a mental trigger. It can be very motivating to tick off an action as complete.

- Use a paper calendar or print out a week from your online calendar and allocate specific tasks to each of the working days. Put the calendar in a prominent place where you know you are going to see it every day, such as your bathroom/your laptop monitor.

- Stubbornness. You have to decide whether you want to pay the price to make this happen. Your personal situation is unique but it can be challenging to take the time out of your day to work on your goals. You have to completely own and manage this project from the start. ***Your circus. Your monkeys***.

> *"It always seems impossible until it is done."*
> *Nelson Mandela*

YOUR PLAN IS NOT WRITTEN ON TABLETS OF STONE.

It should be flexible enough to accommodate any challenges that come along. For example; if your target is to write 5,000 words a week, those words may have to be written in 20 minute timed writing sessions every weekend as opposed to small wins every day.

HOW TO WORK SMARTER AND MORE STRATEGICALLY

The 80/20 Rule.

Do you know about Pareto's Law? 80% of your outcomes, your results and your success will come from 20% of your actions.

Your time is limited. You know what you have to do now. So focus on the 20% which will give you the results you are looking for.

This can be very hard. Especially is there is more than one project you want to work on and you have to decide which 80% you must put to one side.

For example; let's say that you have finished your first paranormal erotic romance and you are thinking of self-publishing it.

You will have to do all of the promotion and organise and pay for copyediting, book covers and formatting, or learn these techniques to a professional standard. This is a huge investment in time and money. But you could have your book available for sale online and generating income in eight weeks.

But then you pitch the idea for this story to a literary agent at a romance writers' conference and she is interested in reading the opening chapters!

Brilliant! If the agent loves it and if they can make an editor at a traditional publishing house accept the submission, then you will receive an advance on royalties and your book should be in bookstores for sale in print in 18 months or so, depending on the publisher.

Which option should you take?

Self-publish in eight weeks, or wait for a traditional publisher to pay you an advance and publish your romance some 18 months down the line?

Your final destination has to guide you on every decision you take on how to spend your time and your career as a published author.

If you dream of seeing your book in print and building an audience with a publisher, then option two fits in with that target end result.

On the other hand if you are happy to learn the skillset necessary to successfully launch and market your self-published book and earn a much higher royalty payment for every sale, than option one is the better fit for your long term career plan.

Your time should be spent writing and building a solid foundation as a professional author.

That means not going down interesting distractions and side projects which can suck days or weeks of your time.

Stay on track and work on projects aligned to your long term end results and you will succeed.

Two challenges to watch out for:

- Perfectionism
- Lack of momentum which makes it difficult to get started

Perfectionism is a killer and can crush your momentum.

So many fiction writers never get past chapter one because they feel that they have to have it word perfect before starting chapter two.

The truth is that professional novelists usually have to completely rewrite chapter one, because when they get to the end of the book, the characters have come to life and have completed their character arc. They may have turned out very differently from the characters you thought they were when you began the book. Since the opening chapters set-up the character in the mind of the reader, you will probably have to change the opening when you create the second draft.

All the time you spent procrastinating on the first chapter will be wasted.

It can be tough, but the best way to progress is to accept that your first draft is going to be a 'discovery draft' and just the start.

Getting it done, really is better than having it perfect.

Lack of momentum can makes it difficult to keep on track. Use a Psychological Trick: Set your daily target low.

This is the best way to break through the fear barrier, and never be intimidated again about making a start and taking action.

Set the daily quota of pages, or the number of words you want to write, at a number you know you can achieve, or you won't get started.

If you set a low target, once you get started and build momentum, there is a very good chance that you will write far more than you planned.

For example. You want to finish the first draft of this book before the kids start the school holidays. This means that you have to write 50,000 words in the next 10 weeks.

Let's work the numbers and work backwards from the end result.

50,000 words in 10 weeks = 5000 words a week.

At five days a week this is 1,000 words a day, or four scrappy pages a day. You probably write 1,000 words in all of the texts and emails you send.

Can you write 5,000 words a week? Of course you can.

Your aim should be to create a series of small wins every day.

That's how you get the words done, keep up the momentum and make sure you can enjoy a great family vacation.

To paraphrase the author Nora Roberts, you can fix a crappy page, but you can't fix a blank one.

THE 2-PART CLEAR SUCCESS SYSTEM

You should now have a strategic plan of the broad steps you need to take to reach your end objective and realise your vision.

Now it is time to make this project happen!

PART 1: THE ONE HOUR AUTHOR. HOW TO USE TIMED WRITING SESSIONS

This simple six-step technique will transform your writing process.

Step #1: CENTERING

This step only takes a few minutes to complete but it can make a world of difference to your results.

For the next hour you are going off grid.

This is your time.

Shut out the external pressure and negativity. One by one, cast off all the negative thoughts, brain chatter, self-doubts and past mistakes, and anything else that *"the lizard brain'* is chattering into your ear whenever you even think about starting something exciting and exhilarating.

Reach down inside, into the calm centre of who you are, and **trust** your instincts and your amazing natural ability.

You already know what you have to do. And you know how to do it.

You learnt the ropes and worked your apprenticeship, and are ready to do the best work of your life.

Stop over thinking*. The planning and dreaming time is over. You've done that bit. You don't need to think about it any longer.

The Centering Process

Get comfortable with your back straight and both feet solid on the floor.

Close your eyes and visualise a swimming pool under a bright hot sun and a warm breeze.

It is all yours.

You get up from your lounger - looking good by the way!

Slowly climb the few steps up the ladder to the diving board and stroll casually forward to the very edge.

Up here the world looks so different. The cobalt blue of the sky is reflected in the rippling warm water of the pool just a few feet below you, and you can smell flowers on the warm breeze, which caresses your face and arms and legs. It is magical up here.

It feels as though this is a new world which you have only discovered for the first time.

It's time to jump off the diving board and show the world what you can do. Come on in, the water's lovely.

The sky truly is the limit.

Step #2: CLARITY.

The worst mistake you can make is to start your writing session without a precise list of things to do in that session.

Take a maximum of five minutes before any writing session to write down on paper what you plan to accomplish and why.

Reconnect with your deep personal motivation, then be very specific about the strategic writing task that you are going to work on in this session.

Example. I want to finish chapter nine where the hero finally reveals why he cannot be with my heroine.

Example. I want to work out how the art thieves could steal the Picasso and get away with it.

STEP #3: TIMED WRITING

This technique has saved me more than once, especially on rush jobs where I have to turn around more than one project in a short time period.

If you take nothing else from this chapter, please try this technique as soon as you can.

The goal is to dive into 20 mins of focused work where your total attention is on the work.

You must use some kind of kitchen or screen timer but be strict and only work for 20 minutes. Total attention and focus. Nothing else.

If someone comes in and interrupts you, you have to start again.

A kitchen timer, or the one on your phone, tablet or pc, will do just fine, but there is a psychological benefit in using a mechanical timer that you have to set to 20 minutes.

AND HERE IS THE KEY. Be ready to write very rough pages.

Nobody is going to read this apart from you. Nobody is judging you or watching you.

Write what you want to write.

Don't worry about your conservative relatives being scandalised by the bondage threesome you have visualised.

No editing or spell checking or reading through and putting things right – just head down continuous writing in one complete session.

I know this is hard for perfectionists but it has to be done.

If you have a problem and need some research, leave a marker and come back to it when your session is finished. You can find the information you need on the internet later. Don't interrupt the writing flow to go and look it up.

This draft is for you.

Put everything you want into that piece of writing.

No inhibition. Just full on enjoyment and delight with words.

And write as fast as you can. You should feel the words are flowing out of your fingertips onto the page/keyboard.

Many writers use pencil or pen and paper since they somehow feel less inhibited than typing into a computer system, and the second shaping draft will then become the typed version.

Try it: pen and paper might work for you.

Why 20 Minutes?

You can set any time you want.

My attention span is so short I know that 20 minutes works. You can use 30 minutes if you like, but after that, you would need a longer break which cuts the focus.

If you do have a distracting thought, or good idea about another project, take a few seconds to jot it down in the margin and capture it before it has time to kick off a trip down a side road, and then get back to the project task that you are working on.

STEP #4: STOP WRITING AND GIVE YOUR CREATIVE MIND SPACE

When the timer or buzzer sounds, quickly finish what you were doing then save the file or close your writing pad and get up and walk around.

Take 5 mins to stretch and let your brain play and freewheel on what you have just been doing.

Let your mind work out what to do next all on its own.

You can make tea, load laundry and do non-thinking tasks. Stroll around the garden.

But there are two rules you cannot break.

NO TALKING. AND ABSOLUTELY NO SCREENS!

You have to protect your writing and make your creativity welcome.

STEP #5: GO BACK TO THE SECOND TIMED WRITING SESSION

Go back to your workspace/sofa/bedroom and take a few minutes to reconnect with the work, reading through and thinking - but not editing or revising, just thinking.

Then dive in again for another 20 minutes of complete focused work giving it your full attention. When the timer beeps, finish what you are doing. Then stop.

STEP #6: WRAP UP AND MAKE NOTES FOR THE NEXT SESSION

For the last 5 minutes save the file and back it up, or put your writing pad or journal in a safe place. If you want to, make a note of the computer word count or number of pages.

Then step away from the work and leave it for the day, or until you can spend another hour repeating the process.

Allow your brain to think through the work in the subconscious for the rest of the day, so that when you come back to it later, problems will seem clearer to resolve and you will be buzzing with new ideas.

This six-step timed writing process is a very simplified version of the _Pomodoro technique that was developed in Italy by Francesco Cirillo in the 1990s_.

Cirillo used a tomato-shaped kitchen timer (hence the name Pomodoro) and found that if he broke tasks into 25-minute sessions, followed by a 5-minute break, he was able to concentrate more fully on the tasks at hand and accomplish a lot more in the limited time he had available. This technique has now been developed into a comprehensive time management system and you can find more information on the official website: http://cirillocompany.de/

The key benefits of the Pomodoro technique include:

- It is designed to make it easy for anyone to work in short periods of dedicated focus where you are totally engrossed in one activity to the exclusion of everything else.
- You can stop after the first 20 minute timed writing session, or combine up to four sessions back to back, before taking a longer physical and mental break.
- All you need is a mechanical timer, paper and a pen or pencil. The physical act of winding up the mechanical timer and the click of the timer, acts as a mental trigger which tells the brain that it is time to start work now.
- Willpower is replaced by a repeatable, automatic process for your writing which will build into a complete writing system.
- If you want to use technology there are a wide range of Pomodoro inspired apps you can use, plus the simple countdown timer you can find on most phones, tablets and computers.
- This technique means that you are back in control of your work. No more distractions or procrastination. You have decided to write for one 20 minute session or two and you do it! This is so empowering.
- It takes the emotion and anxiety out of the writing process. You are going to have self-indulgent fun for the next 20 minutes!

THE ONE HOUR AUTHOR

60 Minute Sequence

- 5 Minutes: Centering into your writing headspace
- 5 Minutes: What do you want to accomplish in this session
- 20 Minutes: Timed writing
- 5 Minutes break: No screens
- Back to work for a second 20 minutes
- 5 Minutes: Stop writing and make notes for the next session.

It has been my experience that combining two 20 minute timed writing sessions, in a one hour sequence, has the greatest impact on both productivity and a sense of momentum.

It is long enough for you to create high quality, in depth work, but short enough to fit into a busy schedule.

Each of the six steps in the One Hour Author sequence is fundamental to making the timed writing technique a success, and I would encourage you not to skip a step to save time, especially the centering and planning steps at the start.

PART 2: CREATING A DAILY WRITING ROUTINE

Schedule 30 minute to 60 minute blocks of writing time in your diary or calendar. We are all super busy with life and work. If you don't schedule the time, then someone or something else will use it.

Your writing time is precious. Schedule your writing sessions as carefully as if they were business meetings with your future self.

Using Physical and Mental Action Triggers to Start a Writing Session

Here is a psychological trick.

If you turn up to the same place at about the same time each day and carry out a specific sequence of actions, then your muscle memory and your brain instantly switch into the headspace of what tasks you normally do in that situation.

Behavioural scientist David Hoffeld uses *"preloaded decisions that link a behaviour with an external reference"*, which researchers in his field have found can increase the likelihood of completing a task. These "action triggers" are simple formulas, Hoffeld explains: *"When X happens, I do Y".*

Think about brushing your teeth, making tea, or when you get into the driver's seat of your car.

The sequence of actions that you take in that situation happen automatically, without you having to consciously think about them.

This is the human brain's way of saving you processing power and decision fatigue.

When you get behind the wheel of your car, your brain automatically says oh yes, time to start driving now.

You have trained your brain to think that way because that specific sequence of physical and emotional events has created a learned response - an automatic behavior.

You can use the same technique to create a mental and emotional association between your writing and a very specific combination of contextual elements, to create a writing process which will become so automatic that you won't have to even think about it.

You can call this a habit, a ritual or a routine, but the result is the same. Your writing process will become an automatic learned response which you can turn on in an instant.

What types of TRIGGER signals are we talking about?

Any combination of physical and mental signs that come together to create an environment that the brain recognizes as a trigger.

For example:

- **Action.** Turning on the ratchet of the kitchen timer to start your Pomodoro timed writing session.

- **A specific location.** A coffee shop, your bedroom or desk, sofa or study, the park or a special spot in the local public library. Whatever works for you. You sit in the same place and do the same things every time. Personally I like to write my first draft with either pen and paper or a notebook computer on a lap tray, propped up in bed against the headboard or lying on the sofa with my feet up with a solid reassuring support for my back and neck. Many writers find that the best place for creating writing is not at their desk where they do the admin and computing, but in a different space which is only for composition. It is worth experimenting with a few locations to find one that works for you.

- **Sensory details**. Smells such as scented candles and the tastes of coffee and chocolate. Perhaps the textures from fabrics and the action of pencil lead in contact with sheets of paper.
- **Sound.** Many authors have a soundtrack for a specific book and use one music playlist or individual album track to act as a trigger to help them dive into an emotional or dramatic moment in the story. Other authors play certain composers or styles of music on repeat until the session is over. Other writers insist on complete silence even if it means putting on noise cancelling head phones so they cannot hear the little cherubs screaming at one another in the garden, or coffee being served.
- **Sight**. A favorite picture, screensaver or collage of pictures and images which creates a unique inspiration for that book.
- **Light.** Daylight if possible. Daylight bulbs are widely available and can really help reset your biorhythm
- **Emotional triggers.** Usually a piece of writing can take you into the emotional headspace where you need to be to create your words. A quote from a poem or song lyrics acts in the same way.

It is the combination of several of these triggers that come together to tell the brain it is time to start work on your project.

EXERCISES FOR STEP FOUR: IMPLEMENTATION

One of the most important things that you can do to increase your productivity is to create a daily ritual to help you focus on what you want to achieve each day, and then stick to it.

Entrepreneurs such as Tim Ferris and Tony Robbins use the power of morning rituals to help them focus on their tasks for the day.

The goals are simple:

- Before you start your work for that day, you take time away from your desk to think through what you want to achieve that day.

- You know what your master power list is and why you want to achieve it. Now you have to write down the top 3 things that will move you forward today, on one of more of those large objectives. If needed, reconnect to the excitement and benefits of working on this project.

- Use paper and pen to write everything down rather than a keyboard or touch screen. Many authors use journals, special diaries or notebooks as "day books".
- Then you work out precisely what you are going to do today. Make a list or mind-map or sketch. Whatever works best for you.
- Decide how much time you can allocate today to the tasks on that list. Can you work in 30 minute or 60 minute timed writing blocks?

Don't be Afraid to follow your Body Clock

Note that we focused on creating a Daily Ritual – not just a morning ritual.

Many people find they work best in the evening or even the early hours of the morning when their home is quiet and they are less likely to be interrupted or distracted.

Plus, many home based entrepreneurs use flexible working hours to maintain a work life balance.

Do important things when you are most alert.

Recognize what time of day works best for you. Not everyone is at their freshest early in the morning before their work day begins.

The human biorhythm system means there are certain parts of the day when you are at your creative best, and this is completely to be expected. Only you know when those are.

Don't be afraid to follow your body clock and if you create your best work at a time other than first thing in the morning, that is your quality time and you should work to protect it.

> *"It's not what you do once in a while, it's what you do day in and day out that makes the difference."* —Jenny Craig

You have created your daily ritual; now it is time to build that ritual over time into a daily habit, which is so automatic you don't even have to think about doing it.

Breaking old habits does not happen overnight, but if you can create a writing ritual before you sit down to start on the six-step timed writing sessions, the combination of those two events has the power to transform your productivity.

You will be astonished at how motivating it can be when you feel you are making real progress in the limited time you have in your day to write.

BONUS CONTENT
Go to http://ninaharrington.com/Bonuses to Download a Free Copy of THE 1-HOUR AUTHOR SUCCESS SYSTEM

STEP FIVE. COMMITMENT

THINKING AND ACTING LIKE AN AUTHOR ENTREPRENEUR

"The people who get on in this world are the people who get up and look for the circumstances they want and if they can't find them, make them." George Bernard Shaw

May I suggest to you that in today's publishing world, every single one of us is an author entrepreneur running a global start-up home business. My fiction is translated into 23 languages, and to date I know they have sold both in print and electronic formats in at least 28 countries around the world.

Every one of those 33 books was created in a tiny home office in my house in a small town in the south of England.

In effect, I am running a global creative business from my home.

I am not alone.

You may not be published yet, but the minute you decide that you are going to write for commercial publication of any type, you become a one person business owner.

- A self–employed sole trader who is running a start-up publishing business.
- You are a professional writer who is paid for what you create. The stakes are high. This work is going to pay the bills.
- You are the boss of you, and this is your business.
- You show up every day, and you show up no matter what.
- You are in this for the long haul.
- You invest time and money to train and master the craft and the business skills you need to take informed decisions.
- You do not over-identify with our work but hold the highest standards while still having fun.

I would recommend any new author or aspiring author to reset their perspective from the very start, to think of themselves as running a small start-up business, even if it is a small side-hustle to your day job.

SIX REASONS WHY IT IS CRUCIAL FOR ALL WRITERS TO BECOME MORE PROLIFIC THAN EVER BEFORE.

1. The vast number of new opportunities for readers to read your work

There has been a tsunami of change in technology and the way you and I have access to the written word.

Fifteen years ago, when I started submitting romance fiction, the majority of books were sold only in print format – paperback or hardback – from bricks and mortar book stores.

To reach the bookstore, each book had to be approved by two levels of gatekeepers between the reader and the writer: a literary agent who agreed to represent your work, and then the publisher who supplied the books to booksellers.

Online book sellers were new. Digital books were very new.

Self-publishing carried the stigma of "vanity press" and was mocked as being the last resort for writers who could not find an agent or publisher who would invest in their work.

Every single one of those facts is no longer true.

2. Technology

The English speaking world has developed an insatiable hunger for the written word, and demands to read those words on every kind of reading device created. Dedicated eBook readers, desktop and laptop computers, tablets, smart phones and devices are everywhere.

3. The rise of Independent Publishing

Self-publishing has been made respectable by the large online booksellers who sell eBook readers and apps such as Amazon, Kobo, Barnes &Noble and Apple.

It is in their interest to offer authors high royalties to publish material directly through them, and on the digital eBook readers that they sell, especially in digital format, where they get the cut the publishers used to receive and readers love them because they drive prices down.

4. Online Distribution and Accessibility

Online booksellers offer the complete range of print titles, at big discounts and free delivery to your home.

And with digital eBooks, you can be anywhere in the world, and as long as you have an internet connection, you can download the book you want in minutes and read it on the device you want.

One of the reasons why sales of erotica and fantasy have soared is that readers can discreetly read their tales of bondage on their commute to work on their eBook reader.

Traditional publishers have created '*digital only*' publishing lines to meet the growing shift in how readers consume literature.

It is astonishing.

5. Removal of Traditional Barriers for authors to serve new readers

There are now more markets for your articles, short stories, novels and manuals than ever before.

Cross-over and multi-genre books are opening up new niche markets which would never have been served before, because the perceived audience was too small or esoteric to be commercially viable.

Snippets to be read on mobile phone? Articles and white papers on Amazon Singles? The market is now open to work of any length.

Many authors are now producing work for several publishers, in several genres at the same time. And writing the books they want to write.

But all of that material creates a very serious problem.

6. Hard economics. You need to write more books and better books to make a living as a writer.

I believe that statement is true whether you write commercial genre fiction as I do, or any other kind of fiction or non-fiction.

Book sellers, of all sorts around the world, are involved in a daily price war.

The proliferation of reading devices and content has created such a deluge of material, that the tidal wave has washed away traditional pricing structures for books.

Bricks and mortar bookshops cannot compete on price and range with online booksellers who can negotiate huge discounts from the publishers. Specialist bookstores are just about hanging on, but they can never stock every book by every author in their speciality.

And we are now in a tough economic climate where books are a luxury item.

Let me give it to you straight.

There is a glut of books, both online and in print, and readers expect to pay either very little for those books or even get them for free.

The days when an author can write one book a year, whether fiction or non-fiction, and generate enough sales through a traditional publishing route are long gone.

Unless you already have a huge fan base that will pay for a hardback printed book, the income per book will be low and increasingly, the sales figures will also be disappointing.

Plus, timing and accessibility is everything. For eBooks it is now well established that if a reader loves one of your books then they will want to purchase other books that you have created, especially if these books are linked in some way.

Those books need to be online and available at that moment.

Because if you don't have books available, then the moment is lost and the reader will move on to the next author who does have a trilogy or series of linked books all ready to be enjoyed at the click of a button.

There has never been a better time to be a writer, but in order to take advantage of these opportunities you need to become more prolific.

You truly do need to be:

- Smarter and more strategic in what you write
- More focused than ever before on the clear vision you have for your future identity.
- Become more productive in the time you have available.

So what is going to hold **you** back from becoming more prolific?

STAYING HUNGRY FOR SUCCESS

You are the only one who can decide on what success looks like. Bestselling author? An authority in your niche? Six-figure income? You decide.

But how badly do you want it?

Are you going to stand back and whine about how hard the work is, or get started on just one 30 minute timed writing session and prove to the only person who matters, that you are a writer – yourself!

Life is short.

The best time to seize the opportunity to be who you truly are, is today. Not tomorrow, or the next day, when life could throw rocks at you. **Today.**

You can do it. Be the boss. Turn up for work. This is your business and you are an entrepreneur.

You own this! You've got this.

Stay sharp. Stay hungry for the success you deserve.

"Do. The. Work. Every day, you have to do something you don't want to do. Every day. Challenge yourself to be uncomfortable, push past the apathy and laziness and fear. Otherwise, the next day you're going to have two things you don't want to do, then three and four and five, and pretty soon, you can't even get back to the first thing. And

then all you can do is beat yourself up for the mess you've created, and now you've got a mental barrier to go along with the physical barriers." – Tim S. Grover, Relentless

HOW TO BUILD COMMITMENT INTO YOUR DAILY LIFE

Use Visual Clues to Connect with Your Deep Motivation

Remind yourself why this project is worth the sacrifices that you need to make to see it through to the end, by using a visual stimulus which boosts motivation every time you see it.

Calendars and charts are great at tracking your progress. Seeing your wordcount increase on a book or other project is super motivating and helps to build forward momentum.

Photographs or images of your ideal destination or reward system are also useful depending on your project.

Create a Daily Writing Routine

Use the Two Part Writing System we went through in the last step to create a writing routine, which will build over a few weeks into an automatic learned writing process, which will transform your productivity.

Integrate this system into your life and there won't be any need to rely on willpower to get the writing done.

BATCHING

Batching is the process of collecting together similar tasks and working on them back to back in one concentrated period of time.

If you are using my version of timed writing sprints, then you can already understand the value of focusing your attention on one kind of work at a time.

Batching takes it the next step, and applies the same concept to any of the tasks we might feel we *must do*, as opposed to want to do.

Switching tasks and multi-tasking kills focus. Batching tasks saves time, energy, and frustration!

BATCH YOUR EMAILS

- Turn off the new message alert so that you are not constantly being distracted with a sound or symbol when a new email has arrived in your Inbox.

- Instead of continually checking your emails, you can process all of your emails in one or two sessions a day of focused activity. If you know that your urgent, work-related, emails arrive after 10am in the morning for example, schedule that time in your diary and then check back later in the day after a couple of timed writing sessions.

BATCH YOUR SOCIAL MEDIA POSTS

- You don't have to post new content or comments on social media every hour. Pop onto Facebook or Twitter etc., during coffee breaks to stay in touch with your readers and followers a couple of times a day, but the activity must not consume your prime writing slots.

- You can write all of your blog posts for the entire week or month in one session and schedule them to go live automatically. Same with a marketing and promotion campaign.

- When you put together your social media strategy, it is essential for you to focus only on those social networks that are best for you and your business. Do not strive to be on every social media platform. That would be a waste of time and energy for little return.

- Set up the blog posts from your Website/blog so they are automatically shared to your selected social media outlets.

BATCH ADMIN AND RESEARCH

Schedule specific times in your diary when you are going to catch up with your admin, accounts or when you need to research more information about a project. Otherwise you will start using these necessary, but routine, tasks as part of your procrastination behaviours.

What are some tasks you might consider batching in order to use your time more productively every week?

TAKE CARE OF YOUR HEALTH

Burnout, exhaustion, stress-induced headaches, painful shoulder and neck muscles and carpal tunnel syndrome are just some of the symptoms associated with sitting in front of a screen for eight hours a day.

When do we stop, in a world where we have instant online communication with everyone, everywhere, 24 hours a day?

Your brain needs downtime just as much as your body needs to move, stretch and re-energize, so that we do not risk damaging our health while we try to be more productive.

You cannot create your best work if you are in discomfort or pain or exhausted.

One of the best things you can do for your writing career is to take planned mental and physical health breaks, and have at least one day a week away from the desk.

But here are a few tips to make every break as enjoyable and refreshing as possible:

- Leave your technology at home and focus on the people who are important in your life.
- Enjoy the moment. Yes, it can take many multitaskers a few days to relax into a new way of spending their time, but the benefits to your mental, physical and emotional health can be enormous.
- The shift in energy and space can really help to get you unstuck when you have thinking time.

Your physical and mental health will thank you for it!

SUMMARY OF THE FIVE STEP MAGIC SYSTEM

Deep Motivation and Crystal Clear Objectives. You have your Power List and know what your final destination looks like.

Acceptance. You have acknowledged and accepted your unique strengths and limitations and know that resistance will be part of your journey but still want to continue. Learn how to lean into your strengths.

Gap Analysis. You work out how to get from where you are now, to where you want to go. What will it cost you in time, energy and money to bridge that gap? Are you willing to pay that price?

Implementation of the Plan. Creating a writing system that works for you. How to use the Timed Writing Method to x5 your daily word count

Commitment to Persistent Daily Action. Not a chore, but a fun experiment where you get to create amazing content and share it with the world.

ENDNOTES

Although I am a PhD scientist with a 40 year interest in biochemistry, productivity is a very complex subject, and I am borrowing heavily from experts in the field. Here are a few of the key reference works that I have used during the research for this book.

James Altucher. Numerous posts on *Medium.com*

Roger Black. *Getting Things Done*. Michael Joseph. 1987

Derren Brown. *Happy*. Bantam Press. 2016.

Jane B. Burka and Lenora M. Yuen. *Procrastination: Why You Do It, What to Do About It*. Reading, MA: Addison-Wesley Publishing Company, 1983.

Dean Burnett. *The Idiot Brain*. Faber and Faber. 2016

Carol S. Dweck. *Mindset*. Robinson 2012

David Eagleman. *The Brain*. Canongate. 2015

Ellis, Albert and William J. *Overcoming Procrastination*. Signet Books. 1977

Tim Ferriss. *Tools of Titans*. Ebury Publishing 2016

Tim S. Grover. *Relentless*. Scribner Book Company 2013

M.Hallett. *"Guest Editorial: Neuroplasticity and Rehabilitation."* Journal of Rehabilitation Research and Development 42 (July-Aug.2005): xvii - xxii.

Robert Kelsey. *What's Stopping You?* Capstone. 2011

A.Pascal-Leone, A.Amedi, F.Fregni and L.B. Merabel. *"The Plastic Human Brain Cortex,"* In Response to the Signals: Annual Review of Neuroscience 28 (*2005*): 379.

Steve Peters. *The Chimp Paradox*. Ebury Publishing 2012

Daniel Pink. *Drive*. Canongate. 2009

Steven Pressfield. *The War of Art*. Black Irish Entertainment. 2012

Tom Rath. *Strengths Finder 2.0*. Gallup Press 2007

Roz Shafran, Sarah Egan and Tracey Wade. *Overcoming Perfectionism*. Constable and Robinson. 2010

Jen Sincero. *You are a Badass*. John Murray. 2013

Colin Turner. *Born to Succeed*. BCA. 1994

Ruby Wax. A Mindfulness Guide for the Frazzled. Penguin.2016

ABOUT THE AUTHOR

Nina Harrington grew up in rural Northumberland, England, and decided aged eleven, that her dream job was to be a librarian because then she could read all of the books in the public library whenever she wanted!

Many years later she took the bold decision to take a career break from working in the pharmaceutical industry to realise her dream of being a fiction writer. No contract, no cash, but a compelling passion for the written word.

Nina writes fun, award winning contemporary romance for the Mills and Boon Modern Tempted / Harlequin KISS lines, single title romantic mysteries, and guides and training courses for authors.

Over 1.4 million of her books have been sold in 28 countries and translated into 23 languages.

When she is not creating stories which make her readers smile, or researching best practices for prolific authors, her hobbies are cooking, eating, enjoying good wine, and talking, for which she has had specialist training.

Find out more about Nina at: http://www.ninaharrington.com.

Printed in Great Britain
by Amazon

81617923R00078